German *Lieder*

The German Library: Volume 42

Volkmar Sander, General Editor

German *Lieder*

Edited by Philip Lieson Miller

Foreword by Hermann Hesse

CONTINUUM · NEW YORK

ML
5 4.6
.H275
1990
15-0672

Feb-1991

1990

The Continuum Publishing Company
370 Lexington Avenue, New York, NY 10017

The German Library
is published in cooperation with Deutsches Haus,
New York University.
This volume has been supported by a grant
from the funds of Stifterverband für die Deutsche Wissenschaft.

Printed in the United States of America

Library of Congress Cataloging-in-Publication Data

German lieder / edited by Philip Lieson Miller ; foreword by Hermann
Hesse.
    p.   cm. — (The German library ; v. 42)
English and German.
ISBN 0-8264-0327-1   — ISBN 0-8264-0328-X (pbk.)
    1. Songs, German—Texts.   2. German poetry.   3. German poetry—
—Translations into English.   I. Miller, Philip Lieson, 1906–
II. Series.
ML54.6.G275   1990 <Case>
782.4'3'0943—dc20   89-39980
                                                            CIP
                                                            MN

Grateful acknowledgment is made to Suhrkamp Verlag for permission to
use "Nicht abgesandter Brief an eine Sängerin (1947)" by Hermann Hesse.
From "Musik" © Suhrkamp Verlag am Main 1976. All rights reserved by
Suhrkamp Verlag Frankfurt am Main.

Contents

vi · *Contents*

FELIX MENDELSSOHN-BARTHOLDY

WOLFGANG AMADEUS MOZART

HANS PFITZNER

MAX REGER

FRANZ SCHUBERT

ROBERT SCHUMANN

RICHARD STRAUSS

Foreword

Unmailed Letter to a Female Singer
Hermann Hesse*

As I have many times heard you sing in oratorios and in *Lieder* recitals, in the concert hall and on the radio, and as I, since the death of my friend Ilona—who, however, represents a certain contrast and counterpart to your kind—have listened to no other singer with such joy, admiration, and respect as you, I take the liberty of writing you these lines after your concert today. Admittedly, I did not like this concert today as much as many earlier ones, for the program seemed to me not at all worthy of your art; you sang even this program, one not cheerily welcomed but simply accepted by me, in your perfect manner that stands up to any criticism, in your matter-of-factly quiet, controlled, noble manner, which derives from a union of a very beautiful, elegant, perfectly trained, and controlled voice with the dignity and simplicity of a reasonable and truthful human being. One cannot and should not, I believe, give greater praise to a female singer. What lyrical criticisms frequently praise in superlatives and commend in female singers—the feeling, the mood, the soulfulness, the warmth, the inwardness, and all such characteristics—seems to me dubious and ambiguous and as of little importance as the singer's more or less pretty figure or wardrobe. To be precise, I hope for and expect of you neither soul nor inwardness

*With kind approval of the poet (1877–1962).

nor feeling nor a golden heart; rather, I assume that all this is present in sufficient measure in the song or aria, in the work of art made up of poetry and music together in other words, and which was provided the work by its creator, and that an increase of it is neither necessary nor fruitful. If a text is by Goethe and the music to it is by Schubert or Hugo Wolf, then I trust that this little work will not lack heart, soul, feeling, and would prefer not to be indebted to the singer's personality for still another of these qualities. Not your close relationship to what was sung, not your emotion regarding the work of art do I desire to hear, but the optimally precise and perfect rendition of what is written on the pages of your score. This should neither be heightened by an addition of feeling nor diminished by a lack of understanding. This alone is what we expect of male and female singers, and it is not little; it is incredibly much and is fulfilled by few, for in addition to God's gift of an estimable voice, it requires not only an extremely precise training and practice but also a significant intelligence, an ability to fully grasp the musical qualities of a work, particularly to recognize it as a whole and not to pick the raisins out of the cake and, with exaggerated emphasis, to present these raisins, which are grateful passages for the virtuoso, at the expense of the whole. To provide a quite crude example: I have frequently heard the work "Ich hab' in Penna einen Liebsten wohnen" from the Italian songbook sung by inexperienced young female singers, and the performers had understood and learned nothing else at all from text and composition of the song except that a triumphant shouting of "Zehn!" in the last verse makes an effect. They sang miserably, but the lowest class of the audience was each time more or less taken in by the "Zehn!" and applauded.

All these things are foregone conclusions and yet in practice are not at all understood in themselves, neither by the singers nor by their listeners nor by some of the critics. But if a female singer performs and truly fulfills these seemingly so simple demands, if she really sings what the composer wrote, if she omits or adds nothing, distorts nothing, gives each note and beat its due, then we are each time simply witnessing a stroke of luck and a miracle and feel a heartwarming gratitude, a gentle satiation as we otherwise usually feel only when we ourselves read or perform a favorite work or conjure it up in memory without there being, in other words, a mediator between the work and ourselves.

This rare luck of being given a present by a mediator who takes away from and adds nothing to the work of art, who is indeed will and intelligence but almost no longer person: the friends of good music owe this to such artists as you. Such artists are more difficult to find for vocal than for instrumental music: precisely for this reason the luck of meeting one of these rare artists is so great. There is even another kind of luck in hearing singing, to be sure, and it can be quite intense: the luck of being courted, conquered, and enchanted by a strong and seductive artistic personality. But such luck is not pure—it has a little to do with black magic, it is schnaps instead of wine and ends with surfeit. This impure kind of musical pleasure seduces and spoils us in two ways: it diverts our interest and love of the work of art to the performer and falsifies our judgment by transporting us, for the sake of the interesting performer, to accept into the bargain that which one otherwise would reject. Even with the most miserable hit, after all, the voice of the sirens retains its magic, but the pure, objective, factual practice of art strengthens and, to the contrary, clarifies our judgment. If a siren sings, under certain circumstances we even let ourselves like bad music. But if you, esteemed one, sing and as an exception once extend your program to doubtful music, then your wonderful performance beguiles me to approve this music; but I feel an uneasiness and something like shame and would like best to fall on my knees and request that you devote your art only to the service of the perfect, which alone is worthy of it.

Now, if I could really post this thank-you and love letter, you could rightly respond that you place little value on being instructed about musical qualities and musical judgment by me, a layman. You would rightly forbid me to express criticism of your program. Certainly, but my letter is not going to be sent, it is merely a monologue and lonely reflection. I am attempting to become clear about something to myself, namely about the origin and meaning of my musical taste and judgment. If I converse at all about art, I do so to be sure as an artist, but not as an art critic and aesthetician, but always as a moralist. What I am supposed to reject in the realm of the arts and at least observe with mistrust, what I in contrast should respect and love is not dictated to me by objective, somehow normed ideas of value and beauty, but by a kind of conscience that is of a moral and not aesthetic nature, and which I, precisely because of that, term conscience and not taste. Conscience is subjective and obligatory only for me myself; I am far from wanting to persuade the world to accept the kind of music I love or, say, to want to spoil its pleasure in the other kind that I cannot take seriously. Very little of what theaters and opera stages play daily may attract me, but I am gladly in agreement with the fact that this entire art world and world art flourish and continue to exist. Not in some future do I seek the blessed utopia where only white but no black magic is practiced, where no bluff or dazzler is played; rather, I must create it for myself alone in that tiny section of the world that belongs to me and can be influenced by me. Among what I love and respect are artists and works that never achieve popularity, and among the works which I do not like, which my conscience or taste rejects, are very famous names and titles. The borders are of course not rigid, they are somewhat elastic: from an artist that my instinct previously rejected I occasionally can discover—but to my surprise and shame—a small work in which he nonetheless fits into my world and kind. And even among quite great, even almost sacrosanct masters, I can for a moment occasionally be shocked by a trace of derailment, of vanity, of carelessness, or of ambitiousness and effect-seeking. As I myself am an artist and know my own works to be full of such suspect passages, full of somber interspersions into the purely intentional, such discoveries, despite their basic horridness, are incapable of making me really confused. Whether there ever really were perfect, completely pure, completely pious masters of human origin who were completely engrossed in the work and service is not a matter for me to decide. Enough that there are perfect works, that through the medium of those masters ever and again a crystal piece of objectified spirit has come into being and has been given to people as a gold touchstone.

My judgment about music values, as stated, does not have the ambition to be aesthetically and objectively *correct* or in any sense authoritative or up-to-date. As a writer, I may allow myself a purely aesthetic judgment only about literature, a kind of art about whose means, craft, and possibilities I know and understand to the degree possible for me. My attitude toward the other arts, particularly toward music, is not governed so much by consciousness as by soulful instincts; it does not consist of acts of intelligence but of hygiene, of the need for a certain cleanliness and beneficial effect, for an air, temperature, and nourishment in which the soul feels well and which in any circumstances facilitates the step from comfort to activity, from calmness to the delight in creating. For me, art pleasure is neither deception nor educative drive; it is a matter of breathing air and nourishment, and when I hear music which excites repulsion in me or music which tastes all too sweet, all too sugared and peppered, I reject it not from deep insight into the essence of the art and reject it not as critic, but do so almost completely instinctively. Which, however, does not at all exclude the fact that this instinct in many instances later stands up to scrutinizing discernment. No artist can live without such instincts and soul hygiene, and each has his own.

But to come back to music: to my perhaps somewhat puritanical art morality—the morality and hygiene of an artist and individualist—there belongs not only a sensitivity of soulful nourishment but also a no less sensitive shyness toward all orgies of the community, particularly whatever has to do with mass soul and mass psychosis. This is the peskiest point of my morality, for around this point lie all conflicts between person and community, between the individual soul and mass, artist and audience, and I as an old man would not at all dare, at this late date, to repeat my commitment were it not for the fact that in a special area, namely in the political area, my sensitivities and instincts, often refuted in a horrifying manner by normal and irreproachable people, had not proved right. Many times I have looked on at how a hall full of people, a city full of people, a country full of people was seized by that intoxication and frenzy in which a unity, a homogenous mass emerges from the many individuals, how everything individual dies and the enthusiasm of unanimity, the confluence of all impulses into a mass drive fills hundreds, thousands, or millions with a feeling of exaltation, a desire for commitment, an abjuration of self, and a heroism which is initially expressed in shouting, screaming, scenes of brotherhood accompanied by emotion and tears, but ultimately ending in war, madness, and bloodbaths. Of this capacity of man to intoxicate himself in shared suffering, shared pride, shared hatred, shared honor, my instinct as individual and artist has always vehemently warned me. Whenever this oppressive feeling of exaltation is noticeable in a pub, a hall, a village, a city, a country, I then become cold and mistrustful, I then shudder and already see the blood flowing and the cities going up in flames, while most people, with tears of enthusiasm and deep emotion in their eyes, are still occupied with cheering and fraternization.

Enough of the political. What would it have to do with art? Well, it indeed has this and that to do with it, it has all manner of things in common with it. For instance, the most powerful and most dismal instrument that politics has, mass psychosis, is also the most powerful and dishonest means of art, and a concert hall or theater certainly offers frequently enough—which is to say, at every successful and brilliant evening—precisely that drama of mass ecstasy, and it is a piece of luck that it can let off steam in traditional applause, possibly even increased stomping and shouts of bravo. Without knowing it, much or most of the audience goes to such events solely for the sake of moments of this intoxication. From the body warmth of the many people, from the stimulations of art, from the advertisements of conductors and virtuosi there arises a tension and increased temperature which affects each person who believes he has succumbed to it by lifting him out of himself—which is to say, it for a while robs him of reason and other disturbing inhibitions and, in a fleeting but strong feeling of happiness, turns him into a mosquito dancing along among a great swarm. Even I have occasionally succumbed to this intoxication and magic, at least in my younger years, have participated in trembling and applause and, together with five hundred or a thousand others, have striven to postpone the approaching awakening and sobering up, the end of the exultation; already standing up and actually ready to leave, through our boisterousness we attempted to once again animate the played-out art outfit. But it did not happen to me very often. And what followed these rapturous events was always that ill feeling that we call bad conscience or being in the dumps.

At such art pleasures, though, whenever I was permitted to experience something good, easily beneficial, and of enduring effect, it was moods and states of mind—states of emotion, of cheerfulness, respect, and the intimation of God—for which the masses and the feeling of being infected were not needed. These conditions following those art experiences that I term genuine have each time not left me for hours, not infrequently even for days; I had not experienced a stupor or excitation, but a communion, purification, and thorough radiation, a heightening and illumination of the feeling for life and mental stimuli.

It is no coincidence that, in a letter to you, I reflect on these two kinds of art magic, these two forms of emotion—the black and the white—of transport and reverence; rather, I thereby return to you and to the admiration and gratitude that I feel for your art. For I have indeed experienced strong manifestations of approval but not that mass hysteria in your concerts. These were, however, usually oratorios in which I heard you, works of spiritual music, and even today custom accords these a special dignity appropriate to a worship service by commending to the listeners respect and quiet demeanor instead of ecstasy, shouting, and clapping. But even the circumstance in which you so particularly love and cultivate this kind of music is, from your point of view, a commitment to reverence instead of to intoxication, to dignity instead of delirium. And even secular music you always performed such that the work and not your person was foremost, and that your singing appealed not to approbation but to reverence.

I will of course not bother you with this long letter that I have been writing for many an hour. The respect for you I owed myself, not you. In the letter I profess views that are not very up-to-date and, as I well know, are part of a past stage of mankind and culture which, according to the belief of the optimists, has been *overcome* but which to me is not thereby devalued. Several decades ago a stage of human history that was overcome and ridiculed with horror even included the Tamerlanes and Napoleons, the predatory wars and blitzkriegs, the mass slaughters of people, the tortures, and we have experienced that this *overcome* stage was simply not yet finished and that all their legendary horror again came to the fore. They are today still at the fore. Thus I remain with my old-fashioned views and assume that some future cultural state will recall them and again be able to use this and that of them. Behind them stands my belief in the beautiful, namely, my belief in the fact that the beautiful is on a par with the true and the good, that it is not an illusion and not a human sham but a form of manifestation of the divine.

1947

Translated by Martha Humphreys

Introduction

Not every great composer is gifted with the special ability to set words to music. This may account for the eternal argument as to the relative importance of poetry and music in song. The song begins with the poem; if the music is an enhancement, a translation, or an interpretation, the two elements might be considered equal, though few of us think of them that way. If on the other hand, in the words of Harry Matthews, "When a composer picks a text to set, he is giving himself an excuse to invent an autonomous musical work that will eventually devour it," a composer might as well write purely instrumental program music, providing the text only as a kind of preface.

Representing these two points of view are two kinds of composer. Those who have made a specialty of song usually fit into the first category—respecting the poet as at least an equal. Schubert, it seems obvious, had a natural feeling for words in poetry, and at his best his music—memorable as it is—can hardly be thought of without the text. Schumann was a "literary" composer, with an appreciation of the best in poetry, but he was not above occasionally altering a poem (or was it faulty memory?) in his setting. Robert Franz—highly esteemed by Schumann, Liszt, and Wagner but largely forgotten today—was meticulous in his settings. But Hugo Wolf was unique in his faithfulness to the accents and line of poetry, at the same time making expressive use of the piano in conveying the whole picture as well as the detail. Brahms, who is often considered to represent the second category, sometimes stretched the prosody out of shape, but his ability to capture the essence of the poem is undeniable. Today a composer feels free to do what he likes with a poem, dismembering, cutting, stretching, and rearranging it beyond recognition. Whether what this produces should properly be called a song is open to question.

German *lieder* did not begin with Schubert, though coming as he did at the moment when great poets were producing eminently settable verses and the piano was in the early stages of its development, his incomparable melodic gifts provided the seed from which the romantic *lied* took root. Beethoven, primarily the instrumentalist and not so sensitive to poetry as Schubert, had already pointed the direction, as indeed had Mozart and Carl Philipp Emanuel Bach. But Schubert's first inspiration was Johann Rudolf Zumsteeg, whose ballads impelled the young composer to try his hand, and his earliest surviving song, *Hagars Klage,* is modeled measure for measure on Zumsteeg's setting of the same text. Many of Schubert's earliest songs, not surprisingly, are ballads. At the same time, his contemporary Carl Loewe, also taking off from Zumsteeg, was embarking on a career longer than Schubert's and dedicated mostly to ballad composing. But Schubert, as we know, was eventually more attracted to lyric poetry, though perhaps this early experience developed a feeling for the dramatic which is often present in his songs.

Schubert, whose ability "to set a menu to music" is a popular myth, is often criticized for setting so many verses by his friends and contemporaries, verses which but for him would long ago have been forgotten. The criticism is unjust, as it does not consider the changing of tastes and expressions over the years. What may seem drab and faded today was not so when it was new. What matters is that the best of those poems were settable, and given Schubert's music they still live. In some cases, modern critics have not been able to adjust themselves, most notably in the case of Wilhelm Müller, poet of *Die schöne Müllerin* and *Winterreise.* Müller was a friend of Heine, who told him he hoped that future generations would remember their names together. If the poetry in Schubert's great cycles now seems simple and naive, it is certainly well made, and it provided just the spark the composer needed. In the songs, it is inseparable from the music.

Similar criticisms have been leveled against Brahms and Strauss. But it is notable that these composers rarely set poems to which they felt justice had already been done. Strauss, indeed, declared that he avoided such duplication (there are a few exceptions). If Daumer and Klaus Groth were favorite poets of Brahms it is easy to understand why, for they inspired some eloquent songs. Wolf so devoted himself to his poets that he composed in periods dedicated successively to them. And his songs were published with the names of the poets as prominent as his own.

What makes a poem suitable for setting? I do not think this question has ever been satisfactorily answered. Some critics insist that it must not be great poetry. Some great poems, we are told, actually resist music because they in themselves are so musical. Goethe's *An den Mond* is a prime example: Schubert set it twice; Goethe's friend Zelter and more recently Hans Pfitzner among many others were not intimidated by it. But while this may not be one of Schubert's masterpieces, it still stands up. Yet, if a considerable proportion of Schubert's 603 songs transfigures less than important poetry, it should not be forgotten that no less than 59 poems by Goethe are included, 6 by Heine, 13 by Klopstock, 31 by Schiller, and 5 by Rückert—all anthology poets. Schubert was at his best when inspired by these men.

Much has been made of Goethe's insensitivity to the songs of Schubert. A group of Schubert's friends, thinking to delight the poet, sent him a sheaf of Goethe settings. In the course of considerable time the songs were returned without comment. The question remains open whether Goethe ever actually saw the music, let alone heard it, for in his old age he was watched over by a "palace guard" unwilling to subject him to the music of an unknown. We do know that Goethe had his theories of how songs should be written, and he had his favorite composers—Reichardt and Zelter—to provide him with settings that he felt did not interfere with his poetry. Loewe visited Goethe in 1820 and, at the poet's request, would have sung his setting of *Erlkönig*, but unfortunately there was no piano.

Ideally, words and music should seem inseparable. Yet many examples could be given of different settings of the same poem, each of which might seem definitive were it not for the others—*Du bist wie eine Blume, Kennst du das Land?*, *Über allen Gipfeln ist Ruh'*, are just a few. In considering the *lieder* of Schubert, Schumann, Brahms, Wolf, and Strauss, it is easy to overlook some of the lesser men who contributed to the repertoire. One thinks of Franz, Mendelssohn, Rubinstein, Jensen, Lassen, Henschel, Lachner, Marschner, Raff, Tomaschek and the more recent Pfitzner, Reger, Schoeck, Knab, and Marx. Not all the composers in our index are of great importance, but it is well to remember how many have been active in the field and in many cases forgotten because they were overshadowed.

For the most part the songs in this anthology were composed for voice and piano. Mahler is a borderline case, for one thinks of his songs in terms of the orchestra. His earliest songs, of course, are exceptions. Other *lieder* by Liszt, Marx, Strauss, and others are well known in orchestration. Perhaps the prime example is Wagner's set of five *Wesendorf-Lieder,* of which actually only *Träume* was orchestrated by the composer; the others were done by Felix Mottl.

My intention in these translations is to convey as nearly as possible the meaning of the original poems. I have not attempted to write poetry. Versified and singing translations rarely if ever say just what the poet meant; they usually require some imagination, adding new thoughts often not even suggested in the original. Since the poem is an integral part of the song—even the vowel sounds are a part of the singer's tone—it is not possible to translate without altering the composition. I have tried to render line by line, word by word, what I found in the original. This is not always possible because of German constructions, and because it is sometimes better to write reasonably smooth English than to adhere faithfully to the original word order. Since the poems and translations are set up on facing pages it is easy for the bilingual reader to compare them.

Finally, my grateful acknowledgment is made to Ruth Mead for helping in the selection of songs for this volume.

P. L. M.

German *Lieder*

Ludwig van Beethoven

Ludwig van Beethoven (1770–1827) was primarily an instrumental composer, and it is customary to underrate his contribution to the literature of *lieder*. Though it was Schubert who fully developed the piano-accompanied song, some of Beethoven's finest *lieder* were composed before Schubert was born: *Adelaide* (1794–95) and *Neue Liebe, neues Leben* (1798–99), for example. When Beethoven and Schubert set the same poems—*Der Wachtelschlag, Wonne der Wehmut*—their approaches were sometimes not too far apart, and in the case of *Kennst du das Land?* Beethoven's song certainly was superior.

Adelaide, op. 46

Einsam wandelt dein Freund im Frühlingsgarten,
Mild vom lieblich Zauberlicht umflossen,
Das durch wankende Blütenzweige zittert,
Adelaide!

In der spiegelnden Flut, im Schnee der Alpen,
In des sinkenden Tages Goldgewölken,
Im Gefilde der Sterne strahlt dein Bildnis,
Adelaide!

Abendlüftchen im zarten Laube flüstern,
Silberglöckchen des Mais im Grase säuseln,
Wellen rauschen und Nachtigallen flöten:
Adelaide!

Einst, o Wunder! entblüht auf meinem Grabe
Eine Blume der Asche meines Herzens;
Deutlich schimmert auf jedem Purpurblättchen:
Adelaide!

Friedrich von Matthison, 1761–1831

(Franz Schubert, D. 95)

Die Ehre Gottes aus der Natur, op. 48, no. 4

Die Himmel rühmen des Ewigen Ehre,
Ihr Schall pflanzt seinen Namen fort.
Ihn rühmt der Erdkreis, ihn preisen die Meere;
Vernimm, o Mensch, ihr göttlich Wort!

Wer trägt der Himmel unzählbare Sterne?
Wer führt die Sonn aus ihrem Zelt?

Adelaide

Alone, your friend is wandering in the springtime garden,
enveloped in the magical soft light
that trembles through the moving, blooming branches,
Adelaide!

In the shimmering tide, in the snow of the Alps,
in the golden clouds of sinking day,
in the field of stars, shines your image,
Adelaide!

The evening breezes whisper through the soft leaves;
silver May bells murmur in the grass;
waves roar it, and nightingales warble it—
Adelaide!

Some day, o miracle! Upon my grave shall bloom
a flower from the ashes of my heart;
clearly it will shine on every purple leaf—
Adelaide!

Nature's Praise of God

The heavens proclaim the glory of the Infinite;
their sound magnifies His name.
The earth praises Him, the sea extols Him:
heed, o man, their God-inspired word.

Who sustains the countless stars of heaven?
Who leads the sun out of its canopy?

Sie kömmt und leuchtet und lacht uns von ferne,
Und läuft den Weg, gleich als ein Held.

Christian Fürchtegott Gellert, 1715–69

(Carl Philipp Emanuel Bach)

Mit einem gemalten Band, op. 83, no. 3

Kleine Blumen, kleine Blätter
Streuen mir mit leichter Hand
Gute junge Frühlings-Götter
Tändelnd auf ein luftig Band.

Zephir, nimm's auf deine Flügel,
Schling's um meiner Liebsten Kleid;
Und so tritt sie vor den Spiegel
All in ihrer Munterkeit.

Sieht mit Rosen sich umgeben,
Selbst wie eine Rose jung.
Einen Blick, geliebtes Leben!
Und ich bin belohnt genung.

Fühle, was dies Herz empfindet,
Reiche frei mir deine Hand,
Und das Band, das uns verbindet,
Sei kein schwaches Rosenband!

Johann Wolfgang von Goethe, 1749–1832

(Johann Friedrich Reichardt, 1809;
Othmar Schoeck, op. 19a, no. 4;
Armin Knab, 1924–46)

It comes and lights us, laughing, from afar,
and goes its way like a hero.

With a Painted Ribbon

Little flowers, little leaves—
strewn for me with a light hand
by the good young gods of spring—
are sporting on an airy ribbon.

Zephir, carry it on your wings,
entwine it around my beloved's dress;
so she will step before her mirror
in all her sprightliness.

She will see herself surrounded
with roses, herself like a young rose.
One look, beloved,
and I am well rewarded.

Feel what this heart experiences,
freely give me your hand,
and may the bond that binds us
be no frail rosy ribbon!

Neue Liebe, neues Leben, op. 75, no. 2

Herz, mein Herz, was soll das geben?
Was bedränget dich so sehr?
Welch ein fremdes neues Leben?
Ich erkenne dich nicht mehr.
Weg ist alles, was du liebtest,
Weg, warum du dich betrübtest,
Weg dein Fleiß und deine Ruh—
Ach, wie kamst du nur dazu!

Fesselt dich die Jugendblüte,
Diese liebliche Gestalt,
Dieser Blick voll Treu und Güte
Mit unendlicher Gewalt?
Will ich rasch mich ihr entziehen,
Mich ermannen, ihr entfliehen,
Führet mich im Augenblick,
Ach, mein Weg zu ihr zurück.

Und an diesem Zauberfädchen,
Das sich nicht zerreissen läßt,
Hält das liebe, lose Mädchen
Mich so wider Willen fest;
Muß in ihrem Zauberkreise
Leben nun auf ihre Weise.
Die Verändrung, ach, wie groß!
Liebe! Liebe! Laß mich los!

Johann Wolfgang von Goethe, 1749–1832

Der Wachtelschlag, WoO 129

Horch, wie schallt's dorten so lieblich hervor!
Fürchte Gott! ruft mir die Wachtel ins Ohr.

New Love, New Life

Heart, my heart, what can be the matter?
What oppresses you so?
What a strange new life!
I don't know you any more.
Gone is everything that you loved,
gone the cause of your sadness,
gone your eagerness and your peace—
Ah, how ever did you come to this!

Are you caught in the bloom of youth
by this lovely figure,
this glance full of truth and goodness,
with endless power?
If I want to escape from her quickly,
to take a stand, to flee from her,
she leads me back in an instant;
ah, my way leads back to her.

And by this magic thread
that will not be broken,
the dear inconstant maiden
holds me fast against my will.
I must live in her magic circle
now according to her way.
The change, ah, how great!
Love, love, let me go!

The Call of the Quail

Hark, how lovely it sounds forth yonder:
Fear God! the quail call rings in my ear.

Sitzend im Grünen, von Halmen umhüllt,
Mahnt sie den Horcher am Saatengefild:
Liebe Gott! Er ist so gütig und mild.

Wieder bedeutet ihr hüpfender Schlag:
Lobe Gott! der dich zu lohnen vermag.
Siehst du die herrlichen Früchte im Feld?
Nimm es zu Herzen, Bewohner der Welt!
Danke Gott! der dich ernährt und erhält.

Schreckt dich im Wetter der Herr der Natur:
Bitte Gott! ruft sie, er schonet die Flur.
Machen Gefahren der Krieger dir bang,
Traue Gott! sieh, er verziehet nicht lang.
Bitte Gott! Traue Gott! Sieh, er verziehet nicht lang.

Samuel Friedrich Sauter, 1756–1846

(Franz Schubert, D. 742)

Wonne der Wehmut, op. 83, no. 1

Trocknet nicht, trocknet nicht,
Tränen der ewigen Liebe!
Ach, nur dem halbgetrockneten Auge
Wie öde, wie tot die Welt ihm erscheint!
Trocknet nicht, trocknet nicht,
Tränen unglücklicher Liebe!

Johann Wolfgang von Goethe, 1749–1832

*(Franz Schubert, D. 260; Robert Franz, op. 39, no. 1; Johann
Friedrich Reichardt)*

Sitting in the green, covered by the stalks,
she reminds the hearer in the seeded field:
Love God! He is so indulgent, so benevolent.

Again the jerky call tells us:
Praise God! who is able to reward you.
Do you see the delicious fruit in the field?
Take it to your heart, inhabitant of the world!
Thank God, who nourishes and preserves you.

Are you alarmed by the weather of nature's God:
Pray to God! she calls, who guards the fields.
If the dangers of the warrior make you anxious,
trust in God! See, He does not abandon you for long!

Delight of Melancholy

Dry not, dry not,
tears of eternal love!
Ah, even to the half-dry eye,
how barren, how dead the world appears!
Dry not, dry not,
tears of unhappy love!

Zärtliche Liebe, WoO 235

Ich liebe dich, so wie du mich,
Am Abend und am Morgen,
Noch war kein Tag, wo du und ich
Nicht teilten unsre Sorgen.

Auch waren sie für dich und mich
Geteilt leicht zu ertragen;
Du tröstetest im Kummer mich,
Ich weint in deine Klagen.

Drum Gottes Segen über dir,
Du, meines Lebens Freude.
Gott schütze dich, erhalt dich mir,
Schütz und erhalt uns beide.

Carl Friedrich Wilhelm Herrosee, 1754–1821

Tender Love

I love you, as you love me,
in the evening and in the morning.
There has never been a day when you and I
have not shared our cares.

And for you and me they were
divided to make them light to carry.
You comforted me in grief,
I wept in your laments.

So God's blessing be upon you,
you, the joy of my life.
May God protect you and keep you for me,
protect and keep us both.

Alban Berg

As the most important of Schoenberg's disciples, Alban Berg (1885–1935) is classed with the atonalists and twelve-tone composers. Like Schoenberg himself, however, he grew up in Vienna during the late Romantic period, and his early songs, some of which have become well known, belong to the generation of Strauss and Mahler.

Die Nachtigall

Das macht, es hat die Nachtigall
Die ganze Nacht gesungen;
Da sind von ihrem süssen Schall,
Da sind im Hall und Widerhall
Die Rosen aufgesprungen.

Sie war doch sonst ein wildes Blut,
Nun geht sie tief in Sinnen,
Trägt in der Hand den Sommerhut
Und duldet still der Sonne Glut
Und weiss nicht, was beginnen.

Das macht, es hat die Nachtigall
Die ganze Nacht gesungen;
Da sind von ihrem süssen Schall,
Da sind im Hall und Widerhall
Die Rosen aufgesprungen.

Theodor Storm, 1817–88

(Reinhold Becker, op. 5, no. 2; Emil Sjögren, op. 16, no. 3; Erik Meyer-Helmund, op. 27, no. 1)

The Nightingale

It was because the nightingale
sang all through the night
that from her sweet sound,
reverberating and echoing,
the roses burst into bloom.

But for that she was a wild young blood;
now she is deeply thoughtful,
carries her summer hat in her hand
and calmly endures the heat of the sun,
and doesn't know what to do.

It was because the nightingale
sang all through the night
that from her sweet sound,
reverberating and echoing,
the roses burst into bloom.

Johannes Brahms

Johannes Brahms (1833–97) was a protégé of Schumann, a great admirer of Schubert, and a symphonist, hailed as the successor to Beethoven. These influences are notable in his music, which is also strongly flavored by his love of folksongs and his lifelong study of the music of former ages. He has been criticized for his choice of poets, for though he set seven of Goethe's poems and six of Heine's, he found inspiration more often in the works of Georg Friedrich Daumer and Klaus Groth. It should be remembered that Goethe and Heine had been generously represented in the *lieder* of his predecessors, and the poetry of Daumer and Groth certainly had the special qualities that make good song texts. He has also been criticized for his sometimes cavalier treatment of the words, for his occasional disregard of correct accentuation, and for breaking phrases. In this he was the antithesis of Hugo Wolf, who so successfully suggested natural speech. But considered as a whole, Brahms's offenses were minor; there can be no question as to his ability for establishing a mood and capturing the essence of a poem.

Am Sonntag Morgen, op. 49, no. 1

Am Sonntag Morgen, zierlich angetan,
Wohl weiss ich, wo du da bist hingegangen,
Und manche Leute waren, die dich sahn,
Und kamen dann zu mir, dich zu verklagen.
Als sie mir's sagten, hab' ich laut gelacht
Und in der Kammer dann geweint zur Nacht.
Als sie mir's sagten, fing ich an zu singen,
Und einsam dann die Hände wund zu ringen.

Paul Johann Ludwig Heyse, 1830–1914

(Hermann Götz, op. 4, no. 5; W. Riedel, op. 2, no. 1)

An die Nachtigall, op. 46, no. 4

Geuβ nicht so laut der liebentflammten Lieder
Tonreichen Schall
Vom Blütenast des Apfelbaums hernieder,
O Nachtigall!
Du tönest mir mit deiner süβen Kehle
Die Liebe wach;
Denn schon durchbebt die Tiefen meiner Seele
Dein schmelzend "Ach."

Dann flieht der Schlaf von neuem dieses Lager,
Ich starre dann
Mit nassem Blick und totenbleich und hager
Den Himmel an.
Fleuch, Nachtigall, in grüne Finsternisse,
Ins Haingesträuch,
Und spend im Nest der treuen Gattin Küsse,
Entfleuch, entfleuch!

Ludwig Heinrich Christoph Hölty, 1748–76

(Franz Schubert, D. 196)

On Sunday Morning

On Sunday morning, dressed in your best,
I know very well where you went.
And many people there were who saw you
and then came to me to tell tales about you.
While they were telling me I laughed lustily;
but in my room I wept that night.
While they were telling me I began to sing,
only to wring my hands raw as soon as I was alone.

To the Nightingale

Do not pour out so loudly your amorous songs'
rich strains
down from the blooming bough of the apple tree,
o nightingale!
With your sweet throat
you reawaken my love;
for already the depths of my soul are stirred
by your melting cry.

Then once again I lie sleepless,
staring up
with tear-filled eyes, pale as death, and haggard,
to heaven above.
Flee, nightingale, into the green shadows,
into the grove,
and in your nest spend your kisses on your faithful wife.
Flee, ah, flee!

An eine Äolsharfe, op. 19, no. 5

Angelehnt an die Efeuwand
Dieser alten Terrasse,
Du, einer luftgebornen Muse
Geheimnisvolles Saitenspiel,
Fang an,
Fange wieder an
Deine melodische Klage!
Ihr kommet, Winde, fernherüber,
Ach! von des Knaben,
Der mir so lieb war,
Frisch grünendem Hügel.
Und Frühlingsblüten unterwegs streifend,
Übersättigt mit Wohlgerüchen,
Wie süß bedrängt ihr das Herz!
Und säuselt her in die Saiten,
Angezogen von wohllautender Wehmut,
Wachsend im Zug meiner Sehnsucht,
Und hinsterbend wieder.

Aber auf einmal,
Wie der Wind heftiger herstößt,
Ein holder Schrei der Harfe
Wiederholt, mir zu süßem Erschrecken,
Meiner Seele plötzliche Regung;
Und hier—die volle Rose streut, geschüttelt,
All ihre Blätter vor meine Füße!

Eduard Friedrich Mörike, 1804–75

(Hugo Wolf, Mörike-Lieder, no. 11)

To an Aeolian Harp

Supported by the ivy-covered wall
of this old terrace,
o mysterious harp
of an aerial muse,
begin,
begin again
your sweet complaint!
Winds, you come from far away,
ah, from the fresh green grave
of the boy
who was dear to me.
And touching the spring flowers along the way,
satiated with fragrance,
how sweetly you oppress my heart,
and gently sigh in the strings,
full of melodious melancholy,
swelling with my longing
and dying away again.

But all at once,
as the wind blows stronger,
a glad cry from the harp
echoes, awakening sweet alarm
suddenly in my soul.
And lo! the full-blown rose, shaken, strews
all her petals at my feet.

Auf dem Kirchhofe, op. 105, no. 4

Der Tag ging regenschwer und sturmbewegt,
Ich war an manch vergeßnem Grab gewesen,
Verwittert Stein und Kreuz, die Kränze alt,
Die Namen überwachsen, kaum zu lesen.

Der Tag ging sturmbewegt und regenschwer,
Auf allen Gräbern fror das Wort: Gewesen.
Wie sturmestot die Särge schlummerten,
Auf allen Gräbern taute still: Genesen.

Detlev von Liliencron, 1844–1909

Botschaft, op. 47, no. 1

Wehe, Lüftchen,
Lind und lieblich um die Wange der
Spiele zart in ihrer Locke, [Geliebten,
Eile nicht hinwegzufliehn!
Tut sie dann vielleicht die Frage,
Wie es um mich Armen stehe;
Sprich: "Unendlich war sein Wehe,
Höchst bedenklich seine Lage;
Aber jetzo kann er hoffen,
Wieder herrlich aufzuleben,
Denn du, Holde,
Denkst an ihn."

Georg Friedrich Daumer, 1800–75 (after Hafiz)

In the Churchyard

The day was rainy and blustery;
I visited many forgotten graves.
Stones and crosses crumbling, wreaths withered;
the names so overgrown they could hardly be read!

The day was blustery and rainy;
frozen on all graves was the word: Departed.
As though dead in the storm, the coffins slept;
on all graves silently it thawed: Recovered.

Message

Drift, breezes, gently and lovingly
around the cheeks of the beloved;
play tenderly in her locks;
do not hasten to leave her.
Should she then, perhaps, ask the question
how I, poor man, fare,
say: "Endless was his suffering,
very grave his condition;
but now he can hope
to come to glorious life again
because you, dear one, are thinking of him."

Dein blaues Auge, op. 59, no. 8

Dein blaues Auge hält so still,
Ich blicke bis zum Grund.
Du fragst mich, was ich sehen will?
Ich sehe mich gesund.

Es brannte mich ein glühend Paar,
Noch schmerzt das Nachgefühl:
Das deine ist wie See so klar,
Und wie ein See so kühl.

Klaus Groth, 1819–99

Feldeinsamkeit, op. 86, no. 2

Ich ruhe still im hohen grünen Gras
Und sende lange meinen Blick nach oben,
Von Grillen rings umschwirrt ohn Unterlaß,
Von Himmelsbläue wundersam umwoben.

Die schönen weißen Wolken ziehn dahin
Durchs tiefe Blau, wie schöne stille Träume;
Mir ist, als ob ich längst gestorben bin
Und ziehe selig mit durch ewge Räume.

Hermann Allmers, 1821–1902

(Charles Ives)

Your Blue Eyes

Your blue eyes hold so still,
I look into their depths.
You ask me what I am looking for?
I see myself restored.

I have been burned by a glowing pair,
the memory is still painful.
Yours are as clear as the sea,
and like the sea, so cool.

Alone in the Fields

I lie still in the tall green grass
and gaze a long time upward—
crickets chirping around me ceaselessly,
heaven's blue miraculously woven about me.

The beautiful white clouds drift yonder
through the deep blue, like lovely silent dreams.
It seems as though I have long been dead,
and am drifting blissfully with them through the eternal spaces.

Immer leiser wird mein Schlummer, op. 105, no. 2

Immer leiser wird mein Schlummer,
Nur wie Schleier liegt mein Kummer
Zitternd über mir.
Oft im Traume hör ich dich
Rufen drauß vor meiner Tür,
Niemand wacht und öffnet dir,
Ich erwach und weine bitterlich.

Ja, ich werde sterben müssen,
Eine andre wirst du küssen,
Wenn ich bleich und kalt.
Eh die Maienlüfte wehn,
Eh die Drossel singt im Wald:
Willst du mich noch einmal sehn,
Komm, o komme bald!

Hermann Ritter von Lingg, 1820–1905

(Hans Pfitzner, op. 2, no. 4; Wilhelm Kienzl, op. 24, no. 2;
Ludwig Thuille, op. 4, no. 2)

Der Jäger, op. 95, no. 4

Mein Lieb ist ein Jäger,
Und grün ist sein Kleid,
Und blau ist sein Auge,
Nur sein Herz ist zu weit.

Mein Lieb ist ein Jäger,
Trifft immer ins Ziel,
Und Mädchen berückt er,
So viel er nur will.

Every Night I Sleep More Lightly

Every night I sleep more lightly;
like a veil my grief
lies trembling over me.
Often in my dreams I hear you
calling outside the door.
No one wakes and lets you in;
I awaken and weep bitterly.

Yes, I will have to die;
you will kiss another
when I am pale and cold.
Before the May breezes blow,
before the thrush sings in the wood,
if you want to see me once again,
come, o come soon!

The Hunter

My lover is a hunter,
and green is his suit,
and blue are his eyes,
only his heart is too far away.

My love is a hunter,
he always hits his target,
and girls are caught
as many as he wants.

Mein Lieb ist ein Jäger,
Kennt Wege und Spur,
Zu mir aber kommt er
Durch die Kirchtüre nur.

Friedrich Halm
(Baron Eligius von Münch-Bellinghausen), 1806–71

Komm bald, op. 97, no. 5

Warum denn warten von Tag zu Tag?
Es blüht im Garten, was blühen mag.
Wer kommt und zählt es, was blüht so schön?
An Augen fehlt es, es anzusehn.

Die meinen wandern vom Strauch zum Baum;
Mir scheint, auch andern wär's wie ein Traum.
Und von den Lieben, die mir getreu und mir geblieben,
Wärst du dabei, wärst du dabei!

Klaus Groth, 1819–99

Liebestreu, op. 3, no. 1

"O versenk, o versenk dein Leid, mein Kind,
In die See, in die tiefe See!"
Ein Stein wohl bleibt auf des Meeres Grund,
Mein Leid kommt stets in die Höh.

"Und die Lieb, die du im Herzen trägst,
Brich sie ab, brich sie ab, mein Kind!"
Ob die Blum auch stirbt, wenn man sie bricht,
Treue Lieb nicht so geschwind.

My love is a hunter,
he knows the way and the path,
but to me he will come
only through the church door.

Come Soon

Why then wait from day to day?
What is to bloom in the garden is in bloom.
Who comes and counts the beautiful blossoms?
There are no eyes to see them.

My eyes wander from shrub to tree;
it seems that also to others it must be like a dream.
And among the others who were true to me and remained,
would that you were one!

Faithful Love

"O sink, o sink your sorrow, my child,
in the sea, in the deep sea!"
A stone will stay at the bottom of the sea;
my sorrow will always rise.

"And the love you bear in your heart,
pluck it out, pluck it out, my child!"
A flower will die when we pick it,
true love not so quickly.

"Und die Treu, und die Treu, 's war nur ein Wort,
In den Wind damit hinaus."
O Mutter, und splittert der Fels auch im Wind,
Meine Treu, die hält ihn aus.

Robert Reinick, 1805–52

Das Mädchen spricht, op. 107, no. 3

Schwalbe, sag' mir an,
ist's dein alter Mann,
mit dem du's Nest gebaut,
oder hast du jüngst
erst dich ihm vertraut?

Sag', was zwitschert ihr,
sag', was flüstert ihr
des Morgens so vertraut?
Gelt, du bist wohl auch
noch nicht lange Braut?

Otto Friedrich Gruppe, 1806–76

Mädchenlied, op. 107, no. 5

Auf die Nacht in der Spinnstub'n
da singen die Mädchen,
da lachen die Dorfbub'n,
wie flink geh'n die Rädchen!

Spinnt Jedes am Brautschatz,
daß der Liebste sich freut.
Nicht lange, so gibt es
ein Hochzeitgeläut.

"And your vow—and your vow—it was only a word,
into the wind with it!"
O mother, though the rock be shattered in the wind,
my vow will withstand it.

The Maiden Speaks

Swallow, tell me,
is it your last year's mate
with whom you have built your nest,
or have you recently
made your first vows to him?

Say, what are you twittering,
say, what are you whispering
so intimately this morning?
Surely you too are
not yet long a bride?

Maiden's Song

At night in the spinning room
the girls are singing.
The village boys are laughing
at how quickly the wheels move!

Each girl is spinning for her trousseau
to please her lover.
Before long, it seems,
there will be a wedding.

Kein Mensch, der mir gut ist,
will nach mir fragen;
wie bang mir zu Mut ist,
wem soll ich's klagen?

Die Tränen rinnen
mir über's Gesicht,
wofür soll ich spinnen?
Ich weiß es nicht!

Paul Johann Ludwig Heyse, 1830–1914

Die Mainacht, op. 43, no. 3

Wann der silberne Mond durch die Gesträuche blinkt
Und sein schlummerndes Licht über den Rasen streut,
Und die Nachtigall flötet,
Wandl ich traurig von Busch zu Busch.

Überhüllet von Laub girret ein Taubenpaar
Sein Entzücken mir vor, aber ich wende mich,
Suche dunklere Schatten,
Und die einsame Träne rinnt.

Wann, o lächelndes Bild, welches wie Morgenrot
Durch die Seele mir strahlt, find ich auf Erden dich?
Und die einsame Träne
Bebt mir heißer die Wang' herab.

Ludwig Heinrich Christoph Hölty, 1748–76

(Franz Schubert, D. 194; Fanny Mendelssohn-Hensel)

No lover wants
to ask after me;
how anxious that makes me—
to whom should I complain?

The tears run
down my cheeks;
what am I spinning for?
I do not know.

The May Night

When the silvery moon gleams through the copse,
and pours his slumbering light over the grass,
and the nightingale warbles,
I wander sadly from bush to bush.

Hidden by the foliage, a pair of doves
coos its delight nearby; but I turn away,
seek deeper shadows
and weep a lonely tear.

When, o smiling image, which like the light of morning
shines through my soul, shall I find you upon the earth?
And the lonely tear
trembles hotter down my cheek!

Meine Liebe ist grün, op. 63, no. 5

Meine Liebe ist grün wie der Fliederbusch,
Und mein Lieb ist schön wie die Sonne;
Die glänzt wohl herab auf den Fliederbusch
Und füllt ihn mit Duft und mit Wonne.

Meine Seele hat Schwingen der Nachtigall
Und wiegt sich in blühendem Flieder,
Und jauchzet und singet vom Duft berauscht
Viel liebestrunkene Lieder.

Felix Schumann, 1854–79

Minnelied, op. 71, no. 5

Holder klingt der Vogelsang,
Wenn die Engelreine,
Die mein Jünglingsherz bezwang,
Wandelt durch die Haine.

Röter blühet Tal und Au,
Grüner wird der Rasen,
Wo die Finger meiner Frau
Maienblumen lasen.

Ohne sie ist alles tot,
Welk' sind Blüt' und Kräuter;
Und kein Frühlingsabendrot
Dünkt mich schön und heiter.

Traute, minnigliche Frau,
Wollest nimmer fliehen,

My Love is Green

My love is green like the lilac bush,
and my love is beautiful as the sun
that shines down upon the bush
and fills it with fragrance and with rapture.

My soul has wings like the nightingale
and moves about among the lilac blossoms;
and drunk with the fragrance, it rejoices and sings
many love-happy songs.

Love Song

More pleasing sounds the song of birds
when the pure angel
who has conquered my heart
walks through the grove.

More brightly bloom valley and meadow,
greener grows the grass,
where my lady's fingers
gather May flowers.

Without her every thing is dead,
faded are the blossoms and the plants;
and no spring twilight
seems to me beautiful and clear.

Dear, lovely lady,
do not ever leave me;

Dass mein Herz, gleich dieser Au,
Mög' in Wonne blühen!

Ludwig Heinrich Christoph Hölty, 1748–76
(as edited by Johann Heinrich Voss)

(Franz Schubert, D. 196;
Felix Mendelssohn-Bartholdy, op. 8, no. 1)

Mit vierzig Jahren, op. 94, no. 1

Mit vierzig Jahren ist der Berg erstiegen,
Wir stehen still und schau'n zurück;
Dort sehen wir der Kindheit stilles liegen
Und dort der Jugend lautes Glück.

Noch einmal schau, und dann gekräftigt weiter
Erhebe deinen Wanderstab!
Hin dehnt ein Bergesrücken sich, ein breiter,
Und hier, nicht drüben geht's hinab.

Nicht atmend aufwärts brauchst du mehr zu steigen,
Die Ebne zieht von selbst dich fort,
Dann wird sie sich mit dir unmerklich neigen,
Und eh du's denkst, bist du im Port.

Friedrich Rückert, 1788–1866

Nicht Mehr zu Dir zu Gehen, op. 32, no. 2

Nicht mehr zu dir zu gehen,
Beschloss ich und beschwor ich,
Und gehe jeden Abend,
Denn jede Kraft und jeden Halt verlor ich.

that my heart, like this meadow,
may bloom in rapture!

At Forty

At forty the mountain has been climbed,
we stand still and look back;
there we see the quiet of childhood
and there the boisterous happiness of youth.

Look once more, and then further refreshed
take up your walking stick!
Yonder stretches a mountain ridge, a broad one,
and here, not there, it goes down.

You no longer need to draw your breath for climbing,
the plain in itself will attract you,
and then, without your noticing, it will slope down,
and before you think it, you will be in port.

Never Again to Go to You

Never again to go to you,
I resolved and I swore it;
and I go every evening,
for I have lost all power and all firmness.

Ich möchte nicht mehr leben,
Möcht' augenblicks verderben,
Und möchte doch auch leben
Für dich, mit dir, und nimmer, nimmer sterben.

Ach rede, sprich ein Wort nur,
Ein einziges, ein klares;
Gieb Leben oder Tod mir,
Nur dein Gefühl enthülle mir, dein wahres!

Georg Friedrich Daumer, 1800–1875

O liebliche Wangen, op. 47, no. 4

O liebliche Wangen, ihr macht mir Verlangen,
Dies Rote, dies Weiße zu schauen mit Fleiße.
Und dies nur alleine ist's nicht, was ich meine;
Zu schauen, zu grüßen, zu rühren, zu küssen!

O Sonne der Wonne! O Wonne der Sonne!
O Augen, so saugen das Licht meiner Augen.
O englische Sinnen! O himmlisch Beginnen!
O Himmel auf Erden, magst du mir nicht werden.

O Schönste der Schönen, benimm mir dies Sehnen,
Komm, eile, komm, komme, du Süße, du Fromme!
Ach, Schwester, ich sterbe, ich sterb, ich verderbe,
Komm, komme, komm, eile, benimm mir dies Sehnen,
O Schönste der Schönen!

Paul Fleming, 1609–40

I do not want to live any more,
I wish I could perish right now;
and yet I also want to live
for you, with you, and never, never die.

Ah speak, speak only one word,
a solitary, clear word;
give me life or death,
only let me know your feeling, your true feeling!

O Lovely Cheeks

O lovely cheeks, you make me want
to gaze devotedly at this red and this white.
And this is not all that I mean;
to gaze, to greet, to touch, to kiss!

O sun of bliss! O delight of the sun!
O eyes that drink the light of my eyes.
O angelic thoughts! O heavenly beginning!
O heaven on earth, may you not be mine!

O fairest of the fair, take away my longing,
come, hurry, come, come, sweet innocent!
Ah, sister, I die, I die, I am lost,
come, come, come, hurry, take away my longing,
O fairest of the fair!

O wüßt ich doch den Weg zurück, op. 63, no. 8

O wüßt ich doch den Weg zurück,
Den lieben Weg zum Kinderland!
O warum sucht' ich nach dem Glück
Und ließ der Mutter Hand?

O wie mich sehnet auszuruhn,
Von keinem Streben aufgeweckt,
Die müden Augen zuzutun,
Von Liebe sanft bedeckt!

Und nichts zu forschen, nichts zu spähn,
Und nur zu träumen leicht und lind;
Der Zeiten Wandel nicht zu sehn,
Zum zweiten Mal ein Kind!

O zeig mir doch den Weg zurück,
Den lieben Weg zum Kinderland!
Vergebens such ich nach dem Glück,
Ringsum ist öder Strand!

Klaus Groth, 1819–99

Ruhe, Süßliebchen, op. 33, no. 9

Ruhe, Süßliebchen, im Schatten
Der grünen dämmernden Nacht,
Es säuselt das Gras auf den Matten,
Es fächelt und kühlt dich der Schatten,
Und treue Liebe wacht.
Schlafe, schlaf ein,
Leiser rauscht der Hain,
Ewig bin ich dein.

O that I Knew the Way Back

O that I knew the way back,
the charming way to the land of childhood!
O why did I seek after fortune
and let go of my mother's hand?

O how I long to go to sleep
undisturbed by any aspirations,
to close my tired eyes,
gently protected by love!

And to seek nothing, to notice nothing,
and only to dream, lightly and softly,
not to see the changing times,
once more to be a child!

O show me but the way back,
the charming way to the land of childhood!
In vain I seek after fortune—
around me is waste land.

Rest, Sweet Love

Rest, sweet love, in the shadow
of the green deepening night;
the grass rustles in the meadows,
the shadows fan and cool you,
and true love watches.
Sleep, go to sleep,
the grove murmurs more softly—
forever I am yours.

Schweigt, ihr versteckten Gesänge,
Und stört nicht die süßeste Ruh,
Es lauscht der Vögel Gedränge,
Es ruhn die lauten Gesänge,
Schließ, Liebchen, dein Auge zu.
Schlafe, schlaf ein,
Im dämmernden Schein,
Ich will dein Wächter sein.

Murmelt fort, ihr Melodien,
Rausche nur, du stiller Bach,
Schöne Liebesphantasien
Sprechen in den Melodien,
Zarte Träume schwimmen nach.
Durch den flüsternden Hain
Schwärmen goldene Bienelein
Und summen zum Schlummer dich ein.

Ludwig Tieck, 1773–1853

(Robert Franz, op. 1, no. 10; Ludwig Spohr, op. 72, no. 18;
Wilhelm Berger, op. 8, no. 1)

Sapphische Ode, op. 94, no. 4

Rosen brach ich nachts mir am dunklen Hage;
Süßer hauchten Duft sie als je am Tage;
Doch verstreuten reich die bewegten Äste
Tau, der mich näßte.

Auch der Küsse Duft mich wie nie berückte,
Die ich nachts vom Strauch deiner Lippen pflückte:
Doch auch dir, bewegt im Gemüt gleich jenen,
Tauten die Tränen.

Hans Schmidt, 1854–1923

Be silent, hidden songs,
and don't disturb her sweetest rest;
the flocks of birds are quiet,
let their loud songs rest.
Close, love, your eyes,
sleep, go to sleep,
in the twilight gleam
I will be your watchman.

Murmur on, melodies,
only rustle, silent brook,
beautiful love fantasies
speak through the melodies;
soft dreams float after them.
Through the whispering grove
swarm golden bees
and buzz you to sleep.

Sapphic Ode

Roses I gathered at night from the dark hedge
exhaled a sweeter fragrance than ever by day;
yet the stirring branches showered heavily
moist dew upon me.

Nor has the fragrance of kisses ever so moved me
as when I gathered them from your lips at night;
Yet on you, too—your soul stirred like the branches—
dropped the dew of tears.

Der Schmied, op. 19, no. 4

Ich hör meinen Schatz,
Den Hammer er schwinget,
Das rauschet, das klinget,
Das dringt in die Weite,
Wie Glockengeläute,
Durch Gassen und Platz.

Am schwarzen Kamin,
Da sitzet mein Lieber,
Doch geh ich vorüber,
Die Bälge dann sausen,
Die Flammen aufbrausen
Und lodern um ihn.

Johann Ludwig Uhland, 1787–1862

(Adolf Jensen, op. 24, no. 6; Conradin Kreutzer, op. 23, no. 4;
Reinhold Becker; others)

Sonntag, op. 47, no. 3

So hab' ich doch die ganze Woche
Mein feines Liebchen nicht gesehn,
Ich sah es an einem Sonntag
Wohl vor der Türe stehn:
　　Das tausenschöne Jungfräulein,
　　Das tausenschöne Herzelein,
　　Wollte Gott, ich wär' heute bei ihr.

So will mir doch die ganze Woche
Das Lachen nicht vergehn,
Ich sah es an einem Sonntag
Wohl in die Kirche gehn:

The Blacksmith

I hear my lover:
he is swinging his hammer—
it roars and resounds,
sounding out
like bells
through the alleys and the square.

By the black chimney
there my lover sits—
but if I go past
the bellows begin to hum,
the flames leap up
and blaze around him.

Sunday

All week long
I haven't seen my sweetheart.
I saw her on a Sunday
standing before the door:
the thousand-times beautiful girl,
the thousand-times beautiful sweetheart,
would to God I were with her today:

All week long
I cannot keep from laughing.
I saw her on a Sunday
going into church:

Das tausenschöne Jungfräulein,
Das tausenschöne Herzelein,
Wollte Gott, ich wär' heute bei ihr!

Johann Ludwig Uhland, 1787–1862

(Max Reger; Erik Meyer-Helmund, op. 6, no. 1; others)

Ständchen, op. 106, no. 1

Der Mond steht über dem Berge,
So recht für verliebte Leut;
Im Garten rieselt ein Brunnen,
Sonst Stille weit und breit.

Neben der Mauer im Schatten,
Da stehn der Studenten drei,
Mit Flöt und Geig und Zither,
Und singen und spielen dabei.

Die Klänge schleichen der Schönsten
Sacht in den Traum hinein,
Sie schaut den blonden Geliebten
Und lispelt: "Vergiß nicht mein!"

Franz Kugler, 1808–58

(Franz Abt, op. 105, no. 4)

Therese, op. 86, no. 1

Du milchjunger Knabe,
Wie schaust du mich an?
Was haben deine Augen
Für eine Frage getan!

the thousand-times beautiful girl,
the thousand-times beautiful sweetheart,
would to God I were with her today!

Serenade

The moon stands over the mountain,
just right for lovers;
a fountain splashes in the garden,
otherwise quiet, far and wide.

Alongside the wall in the shadow,
three students stand
with flute and fiddle and zither,
singing and playing.

The music steals to the fair one,
softly into her dream;
she sees her blond lover
and whispers, "Forget me not!"

Therese

You suckling boy!
Why do you look at me like that?
What kind of question
have your eyes been asking?

Alle Ratsherrn in der Stadt
Und alle Weisen der Welt
Bleiben stumm auf die Frage,
Die deine Augen gestellt!

Eine Meermuschel liegt
Auf dem Schrank meiner Bas':
Da halte dein Ohr d'ran,
Dann hörst du etwas!

Gottfried Keller, 1819–90

(Hugo Wolf; Hans Pfitzner, op. 33, no. 3; H. Sommer, op. 16, no. 2; Christian Sinding; others)

Der Tod, das ist die kühle Nacht, op. 96, no. 1

Der Tod, das ist die kühle Nacht,
Das Leben ist der schwüle Tag.
Es dunkelt schon, mich schläfert,
Der Tag hat mich müd gemacht.

Über mein Bett erhebt sich ein Baum,
Drin singt die junge Nachtigall;
Sie singt von lauter Liebe,
Ich hör es sogar im Traum.

Heinrich Heine, 1797–1856

(August Bungert, op. 32, no. 6; Erik Meyer-Helmund, op. 161; Eduard Lassen; Leo Blech; others)

All the town councilors
and all the wise men in the world
remain silent at the question
put by your eyes!

A seashell lies
in my aunt's cupboard:
hold it up to your ear
and you'll hear something!

Death is the Cool Night

Death is the cool night,
life is the sultry day.
It is growing dark already, I am sleepy:
the day has made me weary.

Over my bed there grows a tree;
in it sings the young nightingale,
she sings of nothing but love.
I hear it even in my dream.

Vergebliches Ständchen, op. 84, no. 4

Guten Abend, mein Schatz,
Guten Abend, mein Kind!
Ich komm' aus Lieb' zu dir,
Ach, mach' mir auf die Tür!
Mach' mir auf die Tür!

"Meine Tür ist verschlossen,
Ich lass dich nicht ein;
Mutter die rät' mir klug,
Wär'st du herein mit Fug,
Wär's mit mir vorbei!"

So kalt ist die Nacht,
So eisig der Wind,
Dass mir das Herz erfriert,
Mein' Lieb' erlöschen wird;
Öffne mir, mein Kind!

"Löschet dein Lieb',
Lass sie löschen nur!
Löschet sie immer zu,
Geh' heim zu Bett zur Ruh',
Gute Nacht, mein Knab'!"

Anton Wilhelm Florentin von Zuccalmaglio, 1803–69

Von ewiger Liebe, op. 43, no. 1

Dunkel, wie dunkel in Wald und in Feld!
Abend schon ist es, nun schweiget die Welt.
Nirgend noch Licht und nirgend noch Rauch,
Ja, und die Lerche, sie schweiget nun auch.
Kommt aus dem Dorfe der Bursche heraus,

A Serenade in Vain

Good evening, my dear,
good evening, my child!
I come in love for you,
ah, open the door for me!
Open the door for me!

"My door is locked,
I will not let you in.
Mother warned me
that if I let you in willingly
all would be over for me,"

The night is so cold,
the wind is so icy,
that my heart is freezing.
My love will be extinguished;
open for me, child!

"If your love is extinguished,
just let it go out!
Just keep on extinguishing it.
Go home to bed, to rest!
Good night, my boy!"

Of Eternal Love

Dark, how dark in the woods and the fields!
It is already evening; now the world is quiet.
Nowhere a light and nowhere smoke,
yes, even the lark is silent now.
Out of the village comes the youth,

Gibt das Geleit der Geliebten nach Haus,
Führt sie am Weidengebüsche vorbei,
Redet so viel und so mancherlei:

"Leidest du Schmach und betrübest du dich,
Leidest du Schmach von andern um mich,
Werde die Liebe getrennt so geschwind,
Schnell wie wir früher vereiniget sind,
Scheide mit Regen und scheide mit Wind,
Schnell wie wir früher vereiniget sind."

Spricht das Mägdelein, Mägdelein spricht:
"Unsere Liebe, sie trennet sich nicht!
Fest ist der Stahl und das Eisen gar sehr,
Unsere Liebe ist fester noch mehr.
Eisen und Stahl, man schmiedet sie um,
Unsere Liebe, wer wandelt sie um?
Eisen und Stahl, sie können zergehn,
Unsere Liebe muß ewig bestehn!"

Heinrich August Hoffmann (Hoffmann von Fallersleben), 1798–
1874 (From the Wendish. Brahms mistakenly attributed the poem
to Josef Wenzig, 1807–76)

Wie bist du, meine Königin, op. 32, no. 9

Wie bist du, meine Königin,
Durch sanfte Güte wonnevoll!
Du lächle nur, Lenzdüfte wehn
Durch mein Gemüte, wonnevoll!

Frisch aufgeblühter Rosen Glanz,
Vergleich ich ihn dem deinigen?
Ach, über alles, was da blüht,
Ist deine Blüte wonnevoll!

bringing his sweetheart home.
He leads her by the willow thickets,
talking a great deal about so many things.

"If you are ashamed and troubled,
ashamed of me before the others,
let our love be broken off as speedily,
as quickly as we first came together.
Let us part in the rain, let us part in the wind,
as quickly as we first came together."

The girl speaks:
"Our love shall not be parted!
Iron is strong and steel very much so;
our love is even stronger.
Iron and steel are shaped in the forge,
but who shall change our love?
Iron and steel can be melted,
but our love shall endure forever!"

How Delightful, O My Queen

How delightful you are, o my queen,
with your gentle graces!
You merely smile—fragrances of spring waft
through my soul, delightfully.

The fresh lustre of the new-born rose—
shall I compare it to yours?
Ah, above everything that blossoms
is your bloom delightful.

Durch tote Wüsten wandle hin,
Und grüne Schatten breiten sich,
Ob fürchterliche Schwüle dort
Ohn Ende brüte, wonnevoll!

Laß mich vergehn in deinem Arm!
Es ist in ihm ja selbst der Tod,
Ob auch die herbste Todesqual
Die Brust durchwüte, wonnevoll!

Georg Friedrich Daumer, 1800–1875

Wie Melodien zieht es mir, op. 105, no. 1

Wie Melodien zieht es
Mir leise durch den Sinn.
Wie Frühlingsblumen blüht es,
Und schwebt wie Duft dahin.

Doch kommt das Wort und fasst es
Und führt es vor das Aug',
Wie Nebelgrau erblasst es
Und schwindet wie ein Hauch.

Und dennoch ruht im Reime
Verborgen wohl ein Duft,
Den mild aus stillem Keime
Ein feuchtes Auge ruft.

Klaus Groth, 1819–99

Through the barren forest I wander
and green shade spreads itself—
though horrible sultriness
endlessly broods there—delightfully.

Let me die in your arms!
In them indeed is death itself—
even though the bitterest pangs of death
rage through me—delightful.

Like Melodies

Like melodies it runs
gently in my mind.
Like spring flowers it blooms
and drifts thither like fragrance.

Yet if a word comes and fixes it
and brings it before the eye,
like a gray mist it fades
and vanishes like a breath.

Nevertheless, there remains in the rhyme
a hidden fragrance,
which softly from the silent bud
can be brought forth by tears.

Wiegenlied, op. 49, no. 4

Guten Abend, gut Nacht,
Mit Rosen bedacht,
Mit Näglein besteckt,
Schlupf unter die Deck:
Morgen früh, wenn Gott will,
Wirst du wieder geweckt.

Guten Abend, gut Nacht,
Von Englein bewacht,
Die zeigen im Traum
Dir Christkindleins Baum:
Schlaf nun selig und süß,
Schau im Traum's Paradies.

Des Knaben Wunderhorn (second stanza by Georg Scherer)

Wir wandelten, op. 96, no. 2

Wir wandelten, wir zwei zusammen,
Ich war so still und du so stille;
Ich gäbe viel, um zu erfahren,
Was du gedacht in jenem Fall.

Was ich gedacht, unausgesprochen
Verbleibe das! Nur eines sag ich:
So schön war alles, was ich dachte,
So himmlisch heiter war es all.

In meinem Haupte die Gedanken,
Sie läuteten wie goldne Glöckchen;
So wundersüß, so wunderlieblich
Ist in der Welt kein andrer Hall.

Georg Friedrich Daumer, 1800–1875

Cradle Song

Good evening, good night,
roofed with roses,
trimmed with carnations,
slip under the cover:
tomorrow morning, if God wills,
you will wake up again.

Good evening, good night,
watched over by angels.
They will show you in a dream
the Christchild's tree:
sleep blessedly and sweetly,
in your dream look on paradise.

We Walked Together

We walked, we two together;
I was silent and you were silent.
I would give a good deal to know
what you were thinking then.

What I thought—unspoken
let it remain! Only one thing I say:
so beautiful was everything I thought,
so heavenly and serene was it all!

In my head the thoughts
rang like golden bells;
so marvelously sweet and lovely
is no other sound in the world.

Robert Franz

In his day, Robert Franz (1815–92) was numbered among the greatest *lieder* composers. Robert Schumann, Franz Liszt, and Richard Wagner were among his enthusiastic admirers. The greatest singers—Lilli Lehmann, Marcella Sembrich, and others—used to feature him on their programs, and critics were unanimous in their praise. Today one rarely hears a Franz song in recital, and even in the studios he is largely forgotten. He was first and last a miniaturist. His *lieder* are beautifully fashioned settings of small-scale lyrics, and they offer no opportunity for the singer to make effects. He was particularly partial to the poems of Heine and captured their irony in a quiet subtle way.

Auf geheimnem Waldespfade (Schilflied), op. 2, no. 1

Auf geheimnem Waldespfade
Schleich' ich gern im Abendschein,
An das öde Schilfgestade,
Mädchen, und gedenke dein!

Wenn sich dann der Busch verdüstert,
Rauscht das Rohr geheimnisvoll,
Und es klaget und es flüstert,
Dass ich weinen, weinen soll.

Und ich mein', ich höre wehen
Leise deiner Stimme Klang,
Und im Weiher untergehen
Deinen lieblichen Gesang.

Nikolaus Lenau (Nikolaus Franz Niembsch von Strehlenau),
1802–50

(Alban Berg; Max Bruch; Edgar Tinel; Charles T. Griffes; others)

Aus meinen grossen Schmerzen, op. 5, no. 1

Aus meinen grossen Schmerzen
Mach' ich die kleinen Lieder;
Die heben ihr klingend Gefieder
Und flattern nach ihrem Herzen.

Sie fanden den Weg zur Trauten,
Doch kommen sie wieder und klagen,
Und klagen, und wollen nicht sagen,
Was sie im Herzen schauten.

Heinrich Heine, 1797–1856

(Hugo Wolf; 20 additional composers)

Song of the Reeds

By a hidden path
I like to steal in the evening light
to the desolate reedy shore,
dearest, and think of you.

Then when the bushes darken,
the rushes rustle mysteriously,
lamenting and whispering,
I cannot keep from weeping.

And it seems to me I hear, lightly wafted,
the sound of your voice,
and in the pond it dies away,
your lovely song.

Out of My Great Afflictions

Out of my great afflictions
I make little songs;
they lift their sounding plumage
and fly to her heart.

They found the way to the beloved,
yet they come back to complain.
They complain and will not say
what they saw in her heart.

Bitte, op. 9, no. 3

Weil' auf mir, du dunkles Auge,
Übe deine ganze Macht,
Ernste, milde, träumerische,
Unergründlich süsse Nacht!

Nimm mit deinem Zauberdunkel
Diese Welt von hinnen mir,
Dass du über meinem Leben
Einsam schwebest für und für.

Nikolaus Lenau (Nikolaus Franz Nimbsch von Strehlenau),
1802–50

(Emil Sjögren, op. 16, no. 2; Anton Rubinstein; Felix
Weingartner, op. 16, no. 6; Leopold Damrosch, op. 5, no. 1;
Curt Sachs; Charles Ives; many others)

Request

Rest on me, dark eyes,
bring your full power into play,
earnest, gentle, dreamy
unfathomable sweet night!

Take, with your magical darkness,
this world away from me,
that over my life
you alone shall hover forever and forever.

Franz Liszt

Franz Liszt (1811–86) was a truly international figure; the most famous of Hungarian composers, he studied in Vienna with Czerny and Salieri, and also met Beethoven there. In 1827 he settled in Paris, and after some wanderings he became court *Kapellmeister* in Weimar. His songs are in several languages but principally in German and French. Some of his settings of Goethe and Heine rank among the best.

Die drei Zigeuner

Drei Zigeuner fand ich einmal
Liegen an einer Weide,
Als mein Fuhrwerk mit müder Qual
Schlich durch sandige Heide.

Hielt der eine für sich allein
In den Händen die Fiedel,
Spielt, umglüht vom Abendschein,
Sich ein feuriges Liedel.

Hielt der zweite die Pfeif' im Mund,
Blickte nach seinem Rauche,
Froh, als ob er vom Erdenrund
Nichts zum Glücke mehr brauche.

Und der dritte behaglich schlief,
Und sein Cimbal am Baum hing,
Über die Saiten der Windhauch lief,
Über sein Herz ein Traum ging.

An den Kleidern trugen die drei
Löcher und bunte Flicken,
Aber sie boten trotzig frei
Spott den Erdengeschicken.

Dreifach haben sie mir gezeigt,
Wenn das Leben uns nachtet,
Wie man's verraucht, verschläft, vergeigt,
Und es dreimal verachtet.

Nach den Zigeunern lang noch schaun
Mußt' ich im Weiterfahren,

The Three Gypsies

I once came on three gypsies
lying in a pasture
as my carriage painfully
crawled through the sandy heath.

The one for his own pleasure held
a fiddle in his hands,
playing in the glow of evening
a happy ditty.

The second held his pipe in his mouth
and contemplated the smoke;
happy, he thus required in all the world
no more of destiny.

And the third slept comfortably,
and his cimbalom hung on the tree;
the wind ran through the strings.
over his heart went a dream.

In their clothes the three wore
holes and colored patches,
yet defiantly they showed
scorn for the fate of the world.

Three ways they showed me,
when life darkens,
how to sleep, smoke, fiddle,
and three times disdain it.

The gypsies I could not help seeing long afterward
as I went on my way—

Nach den Gesichtern dunkelbraun,
Den schwarzlockigen Haaren.

Nikolaus Lenau (Nikolaus Franz Niembsch von Strehlenau),
1802–50

(Anton Rubinstein; Othmar Schoeck, op. 24a, no. 4; others)

Es muß ein Wunderbares sein

Es muß ein Wunderbares sein
Ums Lieben zweier Seelen,
Sich schließen ganz einander ein,
Sich nie ein Wort verhehlen,
Und Freud und Leid
Und Glück und Not
So miteinander tragen,
Vom ersten Kuß bis in den Tod
Sich nur von Liebe sagen.

Oskar Freiherr von Redwitz, 1823–91

(Agathe Backer-Grøndahl, op. 60, no. 5; Carl Bohm, op. 326, no.
10; Max Spicker; Franz Ries)

Die Lorelei

Ich weiss nicht, was soll es bedeuten,
Dass ich so traurig bin;
Ein Märchen aus alten Zeiten,
Das kommt mir nicht aus dem Sinn.

Die Luft ist kühl, und es dunkelt,
Und ruhig fliesst der Rhein;

the dark brown faces,
the curly black hair.

It Must Be a Miracle

It must be a miracle,
two souls in love;
they are bound together,
concealing never a word.
And joy and sorrow,
and good fortune and bad
so bearing together;
from the first kiss until death
speaking only of love.

The Lorelei

I do not know what it means
that I am so sad;
a tale of the olden times
will not go from my mind.

The air is cool and it is growing dark,
and the Rhine flows peacefully;

Der Gipfel des Berges funkelt
Im Abendsonnenschein.

Die schönste Jungfrau sitzet
Dort oben wunderbar,
Ihr goldnes Geschmeide blitzet,
Sie kämmt ihr goldenes Haar.

Sie kämmt es mit goldenem Kamme
Und singt ein Lied dabei;
Das hat eine wundersame
Gewaltige Melodei.

Den Schiffer im kleinen Schiffe
Ergreift es mit wildem Weh;
Er schaut nicht die Felsenriffe,
Er schaut nur hinauf in die Höh'.

Ich glaube, die Wellen verschlingen
Am Ende Schiffer und Kahn;
Und das hat mit ihrem Singen
Die Lorelei getan.

Heinrich Heine, 1797–1856

(Friedrich Silcher; Clara Schumann, 1843; Niels W. Gade;
Joachim Raff, op. 98, no. 26; Richard Trunk, op. 90, no. 2;
others)

the peak of the mountain sparkles
in the evening sunlight.

The most beautiful girl is sitting
up over there;
her golden jewels shine,
she is combing her golden hair.

She is combing it with a golden comb
and singing a song
that has a miraculously
powerful melody.

The boatman in his little boat
is seized with sore distress;
he does not look at the rocky reef,
he only looks upward.

I believe the waves
in the end devour the boatman and the boat;
and this, with her singing,
the Lorelei has done.

Carl Loewe

Carl Loewe (1796–1869) was born just two months before Schubert. Like Schubert, he was inspired by the ballads of Zumsteg, but whereas Schubert in time turned to more lyrical types of song, Loewe remained the master of the ballad. He is credited with 368 ballads, though a number of these would be more properly termed *lieder*. He was also a singer and used to perform to his own accompaniment. A less striking melodist than Schubert, he was very skillful in his descriptive piano parts. Loewe's *Erlkönig* is a masterpiece in its own right, and some critics, including Wagner, considered it superior to its famous counterpart. In adhering to Goethe's rhythmic patterns, it is undeniably a more faithful setting.

Prinz Eugen

Zelte, Posten, Werda-Rufer!
Lustge Nacht am Donauufer!
Pferde stehn im Kreis umher
Angebunden an den Pflöcken;
An den engen Sattelböcken
Hangen Karabiner schwer.

Um das Feuer auf der Erde,
Vor den Hufen seiner Pferde
Liegt das östreichsche Pikett.
Auf dem Mantel liegt ein jeder,
Von den Tschakos weht die Feder.
Leutnant würfelt und Kornett.

Neben seinem müden Schecken
Ruht auf einer wollnen Decken
Der Trompeter ganz allein:
"Laßt die Knöchel, laßt die Karten!
Kaiserliche Feldstandarten
Wird ein Reiterlied erfreun!

Vor acht Tagen die Affäre
Hab ich, zu Nutz dem ganzen Heere,
In gehörgen Reim gebracht;
Selber auch gesetzt die Noten;
Drum, ihr Weißen und ihr Roten!
Merket auf und gebet acht!"

Und er singt die neue Weise
Einmal, zweimal, dreimal leise
Denen Reitersleuten vor;
Und wie er zum letzten Male
Endet, bricht mit einem Male
Los der volle kräftge Chor:

Prince Eugene

Tents, watchmen, sentries' calls!
Happy night on the banks of the Danube!
Horses stand around in a circle
fastened to their pegs;
from the narrow saddle-seats
hang heavy carbines.

Around the fire on the ground
before the hooves of his horse
lies the Austrian picket.
Everyone lies on his coat;
on the shakos wave the feathers;
lieutenant and cornet are throwing dice.

Beside his weary dappled horse
rests on a woolen blanket
the trumpeter all alone:
"Leave the dice, leave the cards!
Royal field standards
shall rejoice in a horseman's song.

"The skirmishes of a week ago,
for the benefit of the whole army
I have brought into proper rhyme.
I myself have also set the notes;
therefore, ye white and ye red,
listen, and pay attention!"

And he sang the new melody
once, twice, three times softly
to the horsemen.
And as for the last time he
came to the end, there broke out all at once
the full strong chorus:

"Prinz Eugen, der edle Ritter!"
Hei, das klang wie Ungewitter
Weit ins Türkenlager hin.
Der Trompeter tät den Schnurrbart streichen
Und sich auf die Seite schleichen
Zu der Marketenderin.

Ferdinand Freiligrath, 1810–76

Die Uhr, op. 123, no. 3

Ich trage, wo ich gehe, stets eine Uhr bei mir;
Wieviel es geschlagen habe, genau seh ich an ihr.
Es ist ein großer Meister, der künstlich ihr Werk gefügt,
Wenngleich ihr Gang nicht immer dem törichten Wunsche genügt.

Ich wollte, sie wäre rascher gegangen an manchem Tag;
Ich wollte, sie hätte manchmal verzögert den raschen Schlag.
In meinen Leiden und Freuden, in Sturm und in der Ruh,
Was immer geschah im Leben, sie pochte den Takt dazu.

Sie schlug am Sarge des Vaters, sie schlug an des Freundes Bahr,
Sie schlug am Morgen der Liebe, sie schlug am Traualtar.
Sie schlug an der Wiege des Kindes, sie schlägt, will's Gott, noch
  oft,
Wenn bessere Tage kommen, wie meine Seele es hofft.

Und ward sie auch einmal träger, und drohte zu stocken ihr Lauf,
So zog der Meister immer großmütig sie wieder auf.
Doch stände sie einmal stille, dann wär's um sie geschehn,
Kein andrer, als der sie fügte, bringt die Zerstörte zum Gehn.

Dann müßt ich zum Meister wandern, der wohnt am Ende wohl
  weit,
Wohl draußen, jenseits der Erde, wohl dort in der Ewigkeit!

"Prince Eugene, the noble knight!"
Well, that sounded like a storm
all the way to the Turkish camp.
The trumpeter stroked his moustache,
and slunk aside
to the vivandiere.

The Watch

Wherever I go I carry a watch with me;
how much time it has told I see on it exactly.
He was a great master who skillfully put it together,
even though its working is not always according to my foolish
   wish.

I wished it would go faster on many days;
I often wished that it could slow down its rapid ticking.
In my sorrows and joys, in storm and in rest,
whatever happened in life, it beat the time.

It beat by my father's coffin, it beat at my friend's bier,
it beat in the morning of love, it beat at the marriage altar.
It beat by the child's cradle, it will beat, God willing, many times
   more,
if better times come, as my soul hopes.

And if one time it went slower and threatened to stop,
the master would generously set it going again.
Yet if it stood still, that would be the end,
no one but the maker could put the ruin to running again.

Then I must go to the Master, who lives not far from here,
well out from the earth, way out in eternity!

Dann gäb ich sie ihm zurücke mit dankbar kindlichem Flehn:
Sieh, Herr, ich hab nichts verdorben, sie blieb von selber stehn.

Johann Gabriel Seidl, 1804–75

Die Wandelnde Glocke, op. 20, no. 3

Es war ein Kind, das wollte nie
Zur Kirche sich bequemen,
Und sonntags fand es stets ein Wie,
Den Weg ins Feld zu nehmen.

Die Mutter sprach: Die Glocke tönt,
Und so ist dir's befohlen,
Und hast du dich nicht hingewöhnt,
Sie kommt und wird dich holen.

Das Kind, es denkt: die Glocke hängt
Da droben auf dem Stuhle.
Schon hat's den Weg ins Feld gelenkt,
Als lief' es aus der Schule.

Die Glocke, Glocke tönt nicht mehr,
Die Mutter hat gefackelt.
Doch welch ein Schrecken hinterher!
Die Glocke kommt gewackelt.

Sie wackelt schnell, man glaubt es kaum;
Das arme Kind im Schrecken,
Es lauft, es kommt als wie im Traum;
Die Glocke wird es decken.

Doch nimmt es richtig seinen Husch,
Und mit gewandter Schnelle
Eilt es durch Anger, Feld und Busch
Zur Kirche, zur Kapelle.

Then I would give it back to Him, with thankful, childlike
    entreaty:
See, Lord, I have not damaged it, it stopped of its own accord.

The Walking Bell

There was a child who wouldn't
submit to going to church,
and Sundays he always managed
to take the path into the field.

His mother said: "The bell is ringing,
and so you are summoned;
and if you haven't done as I say
it will come and catch you."

The child thought: "The bell hangs
up there in the frame."
Already he had taken the way into the field
as if he were running from school.

The bell sounded no more—
mother was making it up.
But what a fracas behind him!
here comes the bell, walking!

It walks fast, you'd hardly believe it;
the poor child is terrified.
It runs, it comes as in a dream;
the bell will cover him.

But he seizes the moment
and runs with nimble speed,
runs through the meadow, field and brush,
to church, to chapel.

Und jeden sonn—und Feiertag
Gedenkt es an den Schaden,
Lässt durch den ersten Glockenschlag,
Nicht in Person sich laden.

Johann Wolfgang von Goethe, 1749–1832

(Robert Schumann, op. 79, no. 18)

And every Sunday and feast day,
remembering the fracas,
he doesn't wait for the first peal of the bell
to invite him in person.

Gustav Mahler

Gustav Mahler (1860–1911), the legendary great conductor and director of the Vienna Opera during its Golden Age, has in recent years critically come into his own as a composer. Along with his symphonies, his songs are now a part of the standard repertory, though except for the early ones they are more properly orchestral songs than *lieder*. Although many other composers had drawn on the Armin-Brentano anthology of folk poetry known as *Des Knaben Wunderhorn,* it was Mahler more than anyone else who made these poems famous. And though Friedrich Rückert was a favorite poet with composers from Schubert and Schumann to Brahms and Strauss, perhaps Mahler's settings of Rückert's five poems are the most familiar today.

Ich atmet' einen linden Duft

Ich atmet' einen linden Duft.
Im Zimmer stand
Ein Zweig der Linde,
Ein Angebinde
Von lieber Hand.
Wie lieblich war der Lindenduft!

Wie lieblich ist der Lindenduft!
Das Lindenreis
Brachst du gelinde;
Ich atme leis
Im Duft der Linde
Der Liebe linden Duft.

Friedrich Rückert, 1788–1866

Ich bin der Welt abhanden gekommen

Ich bin der Welt abhanden gekommen,
Mit der ich sonst viele Zeit verdorben;
Sie hat so lange nichts von mir vernommen,
Sie mag wohl glauben, ich sei gestorben!

Es ist mir auch gar nichts daran gelegen,
Ob sie mich für gestorben hält.
Ich kann auch gar nichts sagen dagegen,
Denn wirklich bin ich gestorben der Welt.

Ich bin gestorben dem Weltgetümmel
Und ruh' in einem stillen Gebiet!
Ich leb' allein in meinem Himmel,
In meinem Lieben, in meinem Lied.

Friedrich Rückert, 1788–1866

I Breathed a Gentle Fragrance

I breathed a gentle fragrance;
in the room stood
a branch of linden,
a present
from a dear hand.
How lovely was the fragrance of linden!

How lovely is the fragrance of linden!
The linden bough
that you gently broke;
I breathe lightly,
in the fragrance of linden,
the light fragrance of love.

I Am Lost to the World

I am lost to the world
with which I formerly wasted so much time.
It has for so long heard nothing about me,
that it may well believe that I am dead.

And I do not concern myself about it,
if it believes me dead.
I cannot deny it,
for really I am dead to the world.

I am dead to the tumult of the world
and rest in a quiet domain.
I live alone in my heaven,
in my love, in my song.

Liebst du um Schönheit

Liebst du um Schönheit, o nicht mich liebe!
Liebe die Sonne, sie trägt ein goldnes Haar!
Liebst du um Jugend, o nicht mich liebe!
Liebe den Frühling, der jung ist jedes Jahr!
Liebst du um Schätze, o nicht mich liebe!
Liebe die Meerfrau, sie hat viel Perlen klar!
Liebst du um Liebe, o ja—mich liebe!
Liebe mich immer, dich lieb ich immerdar!

Friedrich Rückert, 1788–1866

(Clara Schumann, op. 12, no. 4)

Rheinlegendchen

Bald gras ich am Neckar, bald gras ich am Rhein;
Bald hab ich ein Schätzel, bald bin ich allein!
Was hilft mir das Grasen, wenn d'Sichel nicht schneid't!
Was hilft mir ein Schätzel, wenn's bei mir nicht bleibt!

So soll ich denn grasen am Neckar, am Rhein,
So werf ich mein goldenes Ringlein hinein.
Es fließet im Neckar und fließet im Rhein,
Soll schwimmen hinunter ins Meer tief hinein.

Und schwimmt es, das Ringlein, so frißt es ein Fisch!
Das Fischlein soll kommen auf's Königs sein Tisch!
Der König tät fragen, wem's Ringlein sollt sein?
Da tät mein Schatz sagen; das Ringlein ghört mein.

Mein Schätzlein tät springen bergauf und bergein,
Tät mir wiedrum bringen das Goldringlein mein!
Kannst grasen am Neckar, kannst grasen am Rhein,
Wirf du mir nur immer dein Ringlein hinein!

Des Knaben Wunderhorn

If You Love for Beauty

If you love for beauty, o do not love me!
Love the sun, for it has golden hair.
If you love for youth, o do not love me!
Love the spring which is young every year.
If you love for treasure, o do not love me!
Love the mermaid, who has many pure pearls.
If you love for love—oh, then love me!
Love me forever, as I will always love you.

Legend of the Rhine

Now I mow by the Neckar, now I mow by the Rhine,
now I have a sweetheart, now I am alone!
What's the good of mowing when the sickle doesn't cut!
What's the good of a sweetheart when she won't stay with me!

So if I must mow by the Neckar, by the Rhine,
I throw in my golden ring.
It floats in the Neckar, it floats in the Rhine,
it will swim at the bottom into the deep sea.

And if it swims, the little ring, a fish will eat it!
The fish will come to the king's table!
The king will ask, whose ring could this be?
Then my sweetheart will say: The little ring belongs to me.

My sweetheart will spring up the mountains and down,
shall bring back to me my gold ring!
You can mow by the Neckar, you can mow by the Rhine
if only you will always throw in your little ring!

Der Tambourgesell

Ich armer Tambourgesell,
Man führt mich aus dem Gewölb.
Wär ich ein Tambour blieben,
Dürft ich nicht gefangen liegen.

O Galgen, du hohes Haus,
Du siehst so furchtbar aus.
Ich schau dich nicht mehr an,
Weil i weiß, i gehör daran.

Wenn Soldaten vorbeimarschieren,
Bei mir nit einquartieren.
Wann sie fragen, wer i gwesen bin:
Tambour von der Leibkompanie.

Gute Nacht, ihr Marmelstein,
Ihr Berg und Hügelein.
Gute Nacht, ihr Offizier,
Korporal und Musketier.

Gute Nacht, ihr Offizier,
Korporal und Grenadier.
Ich schrei mit heller Stimm,
Von euch ich Urlaub nimm.

Des Knaben Wunderhorn

Wer hat dies Liedel erdacht?

Dort oben am Berg in dem hohen Haus,
Da gucket ein feins liebs Mädel heraus.
Es ist nicht dort daheime!
Es ist des Wirts sein Töchterlein.
Es wohnet auf grüner Heide.

The Drummer-Boy

I poor drummer-boy!
They are leading me out of the vault.
If I had remained a drummer
I wouldn't have been captured.

O gallows, o tall house,
you look so fearful.
I won't look at you any more,
because I know that's where I belong.

If soldiers march by
not quartered with me,
when they ask who I was:
Drummer from the lifeguards.

Good night, marble stone,
You mountains and hills,
good night, officers,
corporals and musketeers.

Good night, officers,
corporals and grenadiers.
I cry with a clear voice,
I take my leave of you!

Who Conceived this Little Song?

Over there on the mountain in the great house,
a lovely girl is looking out.
She doesn't live there!
She is the daughter of the innkeeper.
She lives in the green meadow.

Mein Herzle ist wund.
Komm, Schätzle, mach's gsund!
Dein schwarzbraune Äuglein, die haben mich verwundt!
Dein rosiger Mund macht Herzen gesund.
Macht Jugend verständig, macht Tote lebendig,
Macht Kranke gesund, ja gesund.

Wer hat denn das schön Liedlein erdacht?
Es haben's drei Gäns übers Wasser gebracht!
Zwei graue und eine weiße!
Und wer das Liedlein nicht singen kann,
Dem wollen sie es pfeifen! Ja!

Des Knaben Wunderhorn

My heart is sore,
come, darling, make it well!
Your dark brown eyes have wounded me;
your rosy mouth cures my heart.
It makes youth sensible, brings the dead to life,
makes the sick well, yes, well.

Then who conceived this beautiful little song?
Three geese brought it over the water!
Two gray and one white.
And he who cannot sing the ditty,
let him whistle it, yes!

Joseph Marx

Though born and educated in Graz, Joseph Marx (1882–1964) spent his most fruitful years in Vienna as a composer and teacher. His 150 songs are of the late Romantic school, effective for both voice and piano. Several of them have been successfully orchestrated and have enjoyed considerable popularity.

Hat dich die Liebe berührt

Hat dich die Liebe berührt,
Still unter lärmenden Volke,
Gehst du in goldner Wolke,
Sicher von Gott geführt.
Nur wie verloren, umher
Lässest die Blicke du wandern,
Gönnt ihre Freuden den Andern,
Trägst nur nach einem Begehr:
Scheu in dich selber verzückt,
Möchtest du leugnen vergebens,
Dass nun die Krone des Lebens,
Strahlend die Stirn dir schmückt.

Paul Johann Ludwig Heyse, 1830–1914

Marienlied

Ich sehe dich in tausend Bildern,
Maria, lieblich ausgedrückt,
Doch keins von allen kann dich schildern,
Wie meine Seele dich erblickt.

Ich weiß nur, daß der Welt Getümmel
Seitdem mir wie ein Traum verweht,
Und ein unnennbar süßer Himmel
Mir ewig im Gemüte steht.

Novalis (Friedrich von Hardenberg), 1772–1801

*(Franz Schubert, D. 658; Othmar Schoeck, op. 6, no. 5; Artur
Schnabel, op. 11, no. 4; Karl Weigl, op. 8, no. 4; others)*

If Love Has Touched You

If love has touched you,
quietly among noisy crowds
you move in clouds of gold,
securely led by God.
As if lost,
you look around;
leaving others to their pleasures,
you carry only one desire.
Shy even in your ecstasy,
in vain you would deny it,
that now the crown of life
shining adorns your brow.

Song of Mary

I see you in a thousand pictures,
Mary, beautifully portrayed;
yet none of them can depict you
as my soul beholds you.

I know only that the turmoil of the world
then is dispersed like a dream,
and an inexpressible sweet heaven
remains forever in my soul.

Felix Mendelssohn-Bartholdy

One of the great musical prodigies of all time, Felix Mendelssohn (1809–47) was hailed in his lifetime as a composer of the first rank though succeeding generations have tended to underrate him. As a composer of songs, he may never reach the stature of Schubert, Schumann, Brahms, or Wolf, but he may be credited with several masterpieces. His setting of Goethe's *Die Liebende schreibt* outshines both those of Schubert and Brahms, and his music makes Geibel's *Der Mond* worthy of a place among the best of *lieder*.

Auf Flügeln des Gesanges, op. 34, no. 2

Auf Flügeln des Gesanges,
Herzliebchen, trag ich dich fort,
Fort nach den Fluren des Ganges,
Dort weiß ich den schönsten Ort;

Da liegt ein rotblühender Garten
Im stillen Mondenschein,
Die Lotosblumen erwarten
Ihr trautes Schwesterlein.

Die Veilchen kichern and kosen,
Und schaun nach den Sternen empor,
Heimlich erzählen die Rosen
Sich duftende Märchen ins Ohr.

Es hüpfen herbei und lauschen
Die frommen, klugen Gazelln,
Und in der Ferne rauschen
Des heilgen Stromes Welln.

Dort wollen wir niedersinken
Unter dem Palmenbaum,
Und Liebe und Ruhe trinken,
Und träumen seligen Traum.

Heinrich Heine, 1797–1856

(Franz Lachner; Wlhelm Berger, op. 16, no. 3; Wilhelm Taubert,
op. 12, no. 1; others)

Leise zieht durch mein Gemüt, op. 19a, no. 5

Leise zieht durch mein Gemüt
Liebliches Geläute.

On Wings of Song

On wings of song,
beloved, I carry you away,
away to the plains of the Ganges;
there I know the loveliest spot.

There lies a garden in full bloom
in the quiet moonlight;
the lotus flowers await
their dear sister.

The violets titter and flirt
and look up to the stars;
furtively the roses whisper
fragrant tales into each other's ears.

And skipping by and listening
come the gentle, wise gazelles;
and in the distance ripple
the waves of the holy river.

There we will sink down
under the palm tree,
and drink of love and rest,
and dream blissful dreams.

Lightly Moving through My Soul

Lightly moving through my soul
is the sound of bells.

Klinge, kleines Frühlingslied,
Kling hinaus ins Weite.

Kling hinaus, bis an das Haus,
Wo die Blumen sprießen.
Wenn du eine Rose schaust,
Sag, ich laß' sie grüßen.

Heinrich Heine, 1797–1856

(Robert Franz, op. 41, no. 1; Edvard Grieg, op. 48, no. 1; Carl Loewe, 1838; Anton Rubinstein, op. 32, no. 1; many others)

Die Liebende schreibt, op. 86, no. 3

Ein Blick von deinen Augen in die meinen,
Ein Kuß von deinem Mund auf meinem Munde,
Wer davon hat, wie ich, gewisse Kunde,
Mag dem was anders wohl erfreulich scheinen?

Entfernt von dir, entfremdet von den Meinen,
Führ ich stets die Gedanken in die Runde,
Und immer treffen sie auf jene Stunde,
Die einzige; da fang ich an zu weinen.

Die Träne trocknet wieder unversehens:
Er liebt ja, denk ich, her in diese Stille,
Und solltest du nicht in die Ferne reichen?

Vernimm das Lispeln dieses Liebewehens;
Mein einzig Glück auf Erden ist dein Wille,
Dein freundlicher, zu mir; gib mir ein Zeichen!

Johann Wolfgang von Goethe, 1749–1832

(Johannes Brahms, op. 47, no. 5; Franz Schubert, D. 673; August Bungert, op. 2, no. 6; others)

Sound, little song of spring,
sound out into the distance.

Sound out to the house
where the flowers are sprouting.
If you see a rose,
say I send greetings.

Love Letter

A glance from your eyes into mine,
a kiss from your mouth upon my mouth,
to one who has, like me, assurance of these,
can anything else have charm?

Far from you, estranged from my own,
I direct my thoughts constantly around,
and always they meet at that hour,
the only one; then I begin to weep.

Suddenly those tears dry again:
He loves me, I think, here in this silence,
and should you not reach into the distance?

Understand the whisper of this breeze of love;
my only happiness on earth is your will,
your gracious will to me; give me a sign!

Der Mond, op. 86, no. 5

Mein Herz ist wie die dunkle Nacht,
Wenn alle Wipfel rauschen;
Da steigt der Mond in voller Pracht
Aus Wolken sacht—und sieh!
Der Wald verstummt in tiefem Lauschen.

Der Mond, der lichte Mond bist du
In deiner Liebesfülle,
Wirf einen, einen Blick mir zu
Voll Himmelsruh'—und sieh!
Dies ungestüme Herz wird stille.

Emanuel Geibel, 1815–84

(Hans Pfitzner, op. 3, no. 3; Eduard Lassen)

The Moon

My heart is like the dark night,
when all the treetops rustle,
the moon rises in full splendor
gradually from out the clouds, and see,
the woods are hushed, deeply listening!

The moon, the light moon is you
in the fullness of your love;
cast on me one glance full of heavenly repose,
and see: this impetuous heart
will be still.

Wolfgang Amadeus Mozart

The songs of Wolfgang Amadeus Mozart (1756–91) were a minor part of his output, and he himself did not take them too seriously. Nevertheless, his setting of Goethe's *Das Veilchen* was one of the earliest *lieder* with a fully developed piano part. It is also a masterpiece. A number of others also deserve their place in the *lieder* repertoire.

Abendempfindung, K. 523

Abend ist's, die Sonne ist verschwunden,
Und der Mond strahlt Silberglanz;
So entfliehn des Lebens schönste Stunden,
Fliehn vorüber wie im Tanz.

Bald entflieht des Lebens bunte Szene,
Und der Vorhang rollt herab;
Aus ist unser Spiel, des Freundes Träne
Fließet schon auf unser Grab.

Bald vielleicht (mir weht, wie Westwind leise,
Eine stille Ahnung zu),
Schließ ich dieses Lebens Pilgerreise,
Fliege in das Land der Ruh.

Werdet ihr dann an meinem Grabe weinen,
Trauernd meine Asche sehn,
Dann, o Freunde, will ich euch erscheinen
Und will himmelauf euch wehn.

Schenk auch du ein Tränchen mir
Und pflücke mir ein Veilchen auf mein Grab,
Und mit deinem seelenvollen Blicke
Sieh dann sanft auf mich herab.

Weih mir eine Träne, und ach!
Schäme dich nur nicht, sie mir zu weihn;
Oh, sie wird in meinem Diademe
Dann die schönste Perle sein!

Johann Heinrich Campe

Evening Sentiment

It is evening; the sun has set
and the moon shines in silver radiance.
So pass life's most beautiful hours;
they fly past as in a dance.

Soon life's colorful scenes pass by
and the curtain falls.
Our play is over; our friends' tears
are already shed on our grave.

Soon perhaps (it is born to me like the gentle West wind,
a quiet sentiment),
I will end life's pilgrimage
and fly to the land of rest.

Should you then weep beside my grave—
mourning, look at my ashes—
then, o friends, I will appear to you
and waft you heavenward.

You too shed a little tear for me
and pick for me a violet on my grave,
and with a loving glance
look sweetly down on me.

Dedicate one tear to me,
and ah! don't be ashamed to dedicate it;
oh then in my diadem it will be
the most beautiful pearl.

Sehnsucht nach dem Frühling

Komm, lieber Mai, und mache
Die Bäume wieder grün,
Und lass mir an dem Bache
Die kleine Veilchen blühn!
Wie möcht ich doch so gerne
Ein Veilchen wieder sehn,
Ach, lieber Mai, wie gerne
Einmal spazieren gehn!

Zwar Wintertage haben
Wohl auch der Freuden viel;
Man kann im Schnee eins traben
Und treibt manch Abendspiel,
Baut Häuserchen von Karten,
Spielt Blindekuh und Pfand;
Auch gibt's wohl Schlittenfahrten
Aufs liebe freie Land.

Doch wenn die Vögel singen
Und wir dann froh und flink
Auf grünen Rasen springen,
Das ist ein ander Ding!
Jetzt muss mein Steckenpferdchen
Dort in dem Winkel stehn;
Denn draussen in dem Gärtchen
Kann man vor Kot nicht gehn.

Am meisten aber dauert
Mich Lottchens Herzeleid;
Das arme Mädchen lauert
Recht auf die Blumenzeit;
Umsonst hol ich ihr Spielchen
Zum Zeitvertreib herbei,
Sie sitzt in ihrem Stühlchen
Wie's Hünnchen auf dem Ei.

Yearning for Spring

Come, dear May, and make
the trees green again,
and for me by the brook let
the little violets bloom!
How much I would like
to see a violet again,
ah, dear May, how I would like
sometime to go walking!

True, the days of winter have
also many pleasures;
we can trot in the snow,
and in the evening games take over;
we build houses with cards,
play blind man's buff and forfeits;
also there are sleighrides
into the open country.

But when the birds sing
and we then, happy and agile,
leap on the green grass,
that is another thing!
Now my hobby horse
must stand in the corner,
for outside in the garden
we cannot walk, because of the mud.

But most important remains for me
Lotte's sorrow;
the poor girl waits in the garden
for the time of flowers.
In vain I bring her toys
to pass the time away;
she sits in her little chair
like a hen on her eggs.

Ach, wenn's doch erst gelinder
Und grüner draussen wär!
Komm, lieber Mai, wir Kinder,
Wir bitten dich gar sehr!
O komm und bring vor allen
Uns viele Veilchen mit,
Bring auch viel Nachtigallen
Und schöne Kuckucks mit!

Christian Adolf Overbeck, 1755–1821

Das Veilchen

Ein Veilchen auf der Wiese stand
Gebückt in sich und unbekannt:
Es war ein herzigs Veilchen!
Da kam ein' junge Schäferin
Mit leichtem Schritt und munterm Sinn
Daher, daher,
Die Wiese her und sang.

Ach! denkt das Veilchen, Wär ich nur
Die schönste Blume der Natur,
Ach! nur ein kleines Weilchen,
Bis mich das Liebchen abgepflückt
Und an dem Busen matt gedrückt,
Ach nur, ach nur
Ein Viertelstündchen lang!

Ach, aber ach! das Mädchen kam
Und nicht in acht das Veilchen nahm,
Ertrat das arme Veilchen.
Es sank und starb and freut sich noch:
"Und sterb ich denn, so sterb ich doch

Ah, if it were only milder
and greener outside!
Come, dear May, we children
beg you so earnestly!
O come and above all bring
many violets for us;
bring also the nightingales
and beautiful cuckoos!

The Violet

A violet stood in the meadow,
modest and unknown;
it was a charming violet.
There came a young shepherdess,
light of foot and merry of heart,
this way, this way
along the meadow, singing.

"Ah," thought the violet, "if I were only
the most beautiful flower in nature,
ah, only for a little while,
so that the sweet one might pick me
and press me till faint on her bosom!
Ah, only, only
for a quarter of an hour!"

Ah, but ah! the maiden came
and not noticing it
stepped on the poor violet.
It sank and died, and still rejoiced:
"Even though I die, yet I die

Durch sie, durch sie, zu ihren Füßen doch!"
(Das arme Veilchen! es war ein herzigs Veilchen!)

Johann Wolfgang von Goethe, 1749–1832

(Johann Friedrich Reichardt; Clara Schumann, 1853; Nicolai Medtner, op. 18, no. 5

because of her, because of her,
right at her feet."
(The poor violet! It was a charming violet!)

Hans Pfitzner

Hans Pfitzner (1869-1949) was a prophet with honor in his own land but little appreciated elsewhere. Perhaps best known for his opera *Palestrina*, he composed in many forms. In his early days, he was considered a modernist along with Richard Strauss, but actually his style was conservative. He does, however, deserve a place as a *lieder* composer of the late Romantic period. His tastes in poetry were traditional, with a special leaning toward Eichendorff.

Ist der Himmel darum im Lenz so blau?

Ist der Himmel darum im Lenz so blau,
Weil er über die blumige Erde schau,
Oder ist die Erde so blumig im Lenz,
Weil darüber der rosige Himmel blaut?

Hab' ich dich darum, mein Kind, so lieb,
Weil du gar so lieblich und reizend bist,
Oder bist du darum so reizend, mein Kind,
Weil die Lieb dir ins Herz kommen ist?

R. Leander

Is the Heaven so Blue in Spring?

Is the heaven so blue in spring
Because it looks down on the blooming earth,
Or is the earth in bloom in the spring
Because the roseate heaven turns blue?

Do I love you so much, my child,
Because you are so lovely and charming,
Or are you so charming, my child,
Because love has come to your heart?

Max Reger

Max Reger (1873–1916) remains a controversial figure; his long list of compositions in many forms remains largely unknown. His reputation for ponderousness perhaps has discouraged potential interest. But in the field of song, this is by no means justified. He composed over 250 approachable and often charming songs, 51 in a series he called *Schlichte Weisen*. His one really well-known song, *Mariä Wiegenlied,* is a good example.

Mariä Wiegenlied

Maria sitzt im Rosenhag
Und wiegt ihr Jesuskind,
Durch die Blätter leise
Weht der warme Sommerwind.

Zu ihren Füßen singt
Ein buntes Vögelein:
Schlaf, Kindlein, Süße,
Schlaf nun ein!

Hold ist dein Lächeln,
Holder deines Schlummers Lust,
Leg dein müdes Köpfchen
Fest an deiner Mutter Brust!
Schlaf, Kindlein, süße,
Schlaf nun ein!

Martin Boelitz, 1874–1921

Mary's Cradle Song

Mary sits by the rosebush
and rocks her child Jesus.
Through the leaves lightly
wafts the warm summer wind.

At her feet sings
a colorful bird:
Sleep, child, sweetly,
now go to sleep!

Charming is your smile,
charming your happy slumber;
lay your tired head
securely on your mother's breast!
Sleep, child, sweetly,
now go to sleep.

Franz Schubert

It was the good fortune of Franz Schubert (1797–1828) to begin composing at a time when German lyric poetry was ready for musical setting and the piano had been developed to a point at which it could lend color and drama. He did not invent the German *lied,* but he developed it into a full-blown art form. One of the great melodists of all time, he could match great poetry with unforgettable music. At first strongly influenced by the ballads of Zumsteg, he came into his own working with the poetry of Goethe. Other composers like Schumann, Brahms, and Wolf picked up where he left off, but no one equaled Schubert in his balance of quality and quantity.

Die Allmacht, D. 852

Gross ist Jehova, der Herr: denn Himmel und Erde verkünden
Seine Macht! Du hörst sie im brausenden Sturm', in des
   Waldstroms
Lautaufrauschendem Ruf', in des grünenden Waldes Gesäusel;
Sieh'st sie in wogender Saaten Gold', in lieblicher Blumen
Glühendem Schmelz', im Glanz des stern'erhelleten Himmels.
Furchtbar tönt sie im Donnergeroll, und flammt in des Blitzes
Schnellhinzuckendem Flug; doch kündet das pochende Herz dir,
Fühlbarer noch, Jehova's Macht, des ewigen Gottes,
Blickst du, flehend, empor, und hoff'st von ihm Huld und
   Erbarmen!

Johann Ladislaus von Felsö-Eör Pyrker, 1773–1847

Am Grabe Anselmos, D. 504

Daβ ich dich verloren habe,
Daβ du nicht mehr bist,
Ach! daβ hier in diesem Grabe
Mein Anselmo ist,
Das ist mein Schmerz! das ist mein Schmerz!
Seht, wir liebten uns, wir beide,
Und solang' ich bin, kommt Freude
Niemals wieder in mein Herz.

Matthias Claudius, 1740–1815

Am Meer, D. 957, no. 12

Das Meer erglänzte weit hinaus im letzten Abendscheine;
Wir saβen am einsamen Fischerhaus, wir saβen stumm und alleine.

Omnipotence

Great is Jehovah, the Lord, for heaven and earth proclaim His
    power!
You hear it in the raging storm, in the torrent's loud gushing roar,
in the rustling of the verdant wood; you see it in the gold of waving
grain, in the colorful riot of lovely flowers, in the splendor of the
star-lighted heaven. Fearful it sounds in the roll of thunder, and
flames in the quick flash of lightning. Yet your beating heart
    proclaims
even more clearly to you the power of Jehovah, the eternal God.
You look to heaven in supplication, and hope for grace and
    mercy.

By the Grave of Anselmo

That I have lost you,
that you exist no more,
ah! that here in this grave
is my Anselmo,
that is my torment! That is my torment!
See, we loved each other, we two;
and as long as I live, joy will come
never again in my heart.

By the Sea

The broad sea sparkled
in the last rays of the evening;

Der Nebel stieg, das Wasser schwoll, die Möwe flog him und
  wieder;
Aus deinen Augen liebevoll fielen die Tränen nieder.

Ich sah sie fallen auf deine Hand und bin aufs Knie gesunken;
Ich hab von deiner weißen Hand die Tränen fortgetrunken.

Seit jener Stunde verzehrt sich mein Leib, die Seele stirbt vor
  Sehnen;
Mich hat das unglückselge Weib vergiftet mit ihren Tränen.

Heinrich Heine, 1797–1856

(Heinrich Proch, op. 176)

An den Mond, D. 296, 259

Füllest wieder Busch und Tal
Still mit Nebelglanz,
Lösest endlich auch einmal
Meine Seele ganz;

Breitest über mein Gefild
Lindernd deinen Blick,
Wie des Freundes Auge mild
Über mein Geschick.

Jeden Nachklang fühlt mein Herz
Froh' und trüber Zeit,
Wandle zwischen Freud und Schmerz
In der Einsamkeit.

we were sitting by the deserted house of a fisherman;
we were sitting silent and alone.

The mist rose, the water swelled,
the gulls flew back and forth;
from your eyes, overflowing with love,
the tears fell.

I watched them fall upon your hand,
and I sank upon my knee;
from your white hand
I drank the tears.

Since that hour my body wastes away,
my soul dies of longing—
the wretched woman
has poisoned me with her tears.

To the Moon

You fill again bush and valley
tranquilly with bright mist;
for once, at last, you release
my whole soul.

You watch over my fields
soothingly,
like the gentle eye of a friend,
over my destiny.

My heart is filled with every echo
of happy and of troubled times;
I wander between joy and pain
in solitude.

Fließe, fließe, lieber Fluß!
Nimmer werd ich froh;
So verrauschte Scherz und Kuß,
Und die Treue so.

Ich besaß es doch einmal,
Was so köstlich ist!
Daß man doch zu seiner Qual
Nimmer es vergißt!

Rausche, Fluß, das Tal entlang,
Ohne Rast and Ruh,
Rausche, flüstre meinem Sang
Melodien zu,

Wenn du in der Winternacht
Wütend überschwillst,
Oder um die Frühlingspracht
Junger Knospen quillst.

Selig, wer sich vor der Welt
Ohne Haß verschließt,
Einen Freund am Busen hält
Und mit dem genießt,

Was, von Menschen nicht gewußt
Oder nicht bedacht,
Durch das Labyrinth der Brust
Wandelt in der Nacht.

Johann Wolfgang von Goethe, 1749–1832

(Carl Friedrich Zelter, 1812; Hans Pfitzner, op. 18; Moritz Hauptmann; many others)

Flow, flow, dear river!
Never will I be happy,
so quickly merriment and kisses
and fidelity pass by.

Yet once I possessed
that which is so delightful!
That which, to one's torment,
one never forgets!

Rush, river, along the valley,
without rest or quiet;
rush, to my song
whisper melodies,

when in the winter night,
raging, you overflow
or in the splendor of spring
you nourish the young buds.

Happy he who before the world,
without malice, shuts himself off,
holds one friend to his bosom
and enjoys with him

that which, unknown to men,
or not considered,
through the mazes of the breast
wanders in the night.

An die Leier, D. 737

Ich will von Atreus' Söhnen,
Von Kadmus will ich singen!
Doch meine Saiten tönen
Nur Liebe im Erklingen.

Ich tauschte um die Saiten,
Die Leier möcht ich tauschen!
Alcidens Siegesschreiten
Sollt ihrer Macht entrauschen!

Doch auch die Saiten tönen
Nur Liebe im Erklingen!
So lebt denn wohl, Heroen!
Denn meine Saiten tönen,
Statt Heldensang zu drohen,
Nur Liebe im Erklingen.

Franz, Ritter von Bruchmann, 1798–1867 (after Anacreon)

(Paul Mirsch, op. 1, no. 1)

An die Musik, D. 547

Du holde Kunst, in wieviel grauen Stunden,
Wo mich des Lebens wilder Kreis umstrickt,
Hast du mein Herz zu warmer Lieb entzunden,
Hast mich in eine beβre Welt entrückt!

Oft hat ein Seufzer, deiner Harf entflossen,
Ein süβer, heiliger Akkord von dir
Den Himmel beβrer Zeiten mir erschlossen,
Du holde Kunst, ich danke dir dafür!

Franz von Schober, 1798–1883

(E. Kreuz, op. 2, no. 1; E. Siebert, op. 10; O. Starck)

To His Lyre

I want to sing of the sons of Atreus,
of Cadmus will I sing!
But my strings sound
only of love.

I changed the strings about—
would I could change the lyre!—
on the triumphant strides of Alcides
it should spend its power.

But again my strings sound
only strains of love!
So farewell, heroes!
For my strings sound,
instead of threatening with heroic songs,
only strains of love.

To Music

O sublime art, in how many gray hours,
when the wild tumult of life ensnared me,
have you kindled my heart to warm love,
have you carried me away to a better world!

Often a sigh, escaped from your harp,
a sweet, solemn chord from you,
has opened the heaven of better times to me—
O sublime art, I thank you for it!

An Schwager Kronos, D. 369

Spute dich, Kronos!
Fort den rasselnden Trott!
Bergab gleitet der Weg;
Ekles Schwindeln zögert
Mir vor die Stirne dein Zaudern.
Frisch, holpert es gleich,
Über Stock und Steine den Trott
Rasch ins Leben hinein!

Nun schon wieder
Den eratmenden Schritt
Mühsam berghinauf,
Auf denn, nicht träge denn,
Strebend und hoffend hinan!

Weit, hoch, herrlich der Blick
Rings ins Leben hinein,
Vom Gebirg zum Gebirg
Schwebet der ewige Geist,
Ewigen Lebens ahnevoll.

Seitwärts des Überdachs Schatten
Zieht dich an
Und ein Frischung verheißender Blick
Auf der Schwelle des Mädchens da.
Labe dich!—Mir auch, Mädchen,
Diesen schäumenden Trank,
Diesen frischen Gesundheitsblick!

Ab denn, rascher hinab!
Sieh, die Sonne sinkt!
Eh sie sinkt, eh mich Greisen
Ergreift im Moore Nebelduft,
Entzahnte Kiefer schnattern
Und das schlotternde Gebein.

To the Postilion Chronos

Hurry, Chronos!
Forth at a rattling trot!
The way leads downhill;
I am sick and giddy
from your delay.
Oh! Rough as it is,
jog, at full speed,
swiftly into life.

Now back again,
panting, stride
wearily up the mountain!
Up! have done with sluggishness,
upward, striving and hoping!

Far, high, magnificent the view
of life around us;
from peak to peak
the eternal spirit soars,
presaging eternal life.

Along the way the shade of a shelter
draws you aside,
and a glimpse of a maiden's threshold
promises to revive you.
Refresh yourself!—for me also, maiden,
this foaming drink,
the bright, healing glance!

On your way, then, faster downwards!
See, the sun is setting!
Before it sets, before I, the old man,
am seized by the mist in the moor,
before the chattering, toothless jaws
and the shaky skeleton,

Trunknen vom letzten Strahl
Reiß mich, ein Feuermeer
Mir im schäumenden Aug,
Mich geblendeten Taumelnden
In der Hölle nächtliches Tor.

Töne, Schwager, ins Horn,
Raßle den schallenden Trab,
Daß der Orkus vernehme: wir kommen,
Daß bleich an der Tür
Der Wirt uns freundlich empfange

Johann Wolfgang von Goethe, 1749–1832

Auf dem Wasser zu singen, D. 774

Mitten im Schimmer der spiegelnden Wellen
Gleitet, wie Schwäne, der wankende Kahn;
Ach, auf der Freude sanftschimmernden Wellen
Gleitet die Seele dahin wie der Kahn;
Denn von dem Himmel herab auf die Wellen
Tanzet das Abendrot rund um den Kahn.

Über den Wipfeln des westlichen Haines
Winket uns freundlich der rötliche Schein,
Unter den Zweigen des östlichen Haines
Säuselt der Kalmus im rötlichen Schein;
Freude des Himmels und Ruhe des Haines
Atmet die Seel im errötenden Schein.

Ach, es entschwindet mit tauigem Flügel
Mir auf den wiegenden Wellen die Zeit.
Morgen entschwindet mit schimmerndem Flügel
Wieder wie gestern und heute die Zeit,

drunk with the last ray,
drag me—a sea of fire
in my watering eyes—
blinded and staggering,
to the dismal gate of hell!

Sound your horn, coachman!
Rattle at a resounding trot,
that Orcus may know we are coming!
That right at the door
the host may graciously greet us.

To Be Sung on the Water

Amid the shimmer of mirroring waves
glides, like swans, the rocking boat.
Ah, on the soft shimmering waves of joy
the soul glides away like the boat,
for down from the heavens upon the waves
the evening light dances around the boat.

Over the treetops of the grove to the West
the rosy gleam beckons us on;
under the branches of the grove to the East
the iris rustles in the rosy light.
Happiness of the heavens and quiet of the groves
the soul breathes in the blushing light.

Ah, time passes with dewy wings
for me on the rocking waves.
So tomorrow may time fade with its shimmering wings
again, as yesterday and today,

Bis ich auf höherem strahlendem Flügel
Selber entschwinde der wechselnden Zeit.

Friedrich Leopold, Graf zu Stolberg, 1750–1819

(J. W. Kalliwoda, op. 192; J. F. Kittl, op. 4, no. 3; H. Nürnberg,
op. 2, no. 2)

Aufenthalt, D. 957, no. 5

Rauschender Strom,
Brausender Wald,
Starrender Fels
Mein Aufenthalt.

Wie sich die Welle
Am Welle reiht,
Fliessen die Tränen
Mir ewig erneut.

Hoch in den Kronen
Wogend sich's regt,
So unaufhörlich
Mein Herze schlägt,

Und wie des Felsen
Uraltes Erz,
Ewig derselbe
Bleibet mein Schmerz.

Rauschender Strom,
Brausender Wald,
Starrender Fels
Mein Aufenthalt.

Ludwig Rellstab, 1799–1860

(Heinrich Marschner, op. 76, no. 4)

until I, ascending on higher shining wings,
myself shall yield to the changing time.

My Home

Roaring torrent,
blustering forest,
towering rock,
this is my home.

As wave
follows wave,
my tears flow
ever renewed.

As high in their crests
surging they swell,
so ceaselessly
my heart beats.

And like the rock's
ageless ore,
ever the same
remains my grief.

Roaring torrent,
blustering forest,
towering rock,
this is my home.

Dem Unendlichen, D. 291

Wie erhebt sich das Herz, wenn es dich,
Unendlicher, denkt! wie sinkt es,
Wenns auf sich herunterschaut!
Elend schauts wehklagend dann, und Nacht und Tod!

Allein du rufst mich aus meiner Nacht, der in Elend, der im Tod
hilft!
Dann denk ich es ganz, dass ewig mich schufst,
Herrlicher! den kein Preis, unten am Grab', oben am Thron,
Herr Herr Gott! den, dankend entflammt, kein Jubel genug
besingt.

Weht, Bäume des Lebens, im Harfengetön!
Rausche mit ihnen ins Harfengetön, krystallner Strom!
Ihr lispelt, und rauscht, und, Harfen, ihr tönt
Nie es ganz! Gott ist es, den ihr preist!

Donnert, Welten, in feierlichem Gang, in der Posaunen Chor!
Du Orion, wage, du auch!
Tönt all' ihr Sonnen auf der Strasse voll Glanz,
In der Posaunen Chor!

Ihr Welten, donnert
Und du, der Posaunen Chor, hallest
Nie es ganz, Gott; nie es ganz, Gott,
Gott, Gott ist es, den ihr preist!

Friedrich Gottlieb Klopstock, 1724–1803

Des Mädchens Klage, D. 191

Der Eichwald brauset, die Wolken ziehn,
Das Mädchen sitzet an Ufers Grün;

To the Infinite

How my heart leaps when it thinks
on Thee, o Infinite One! How it sinks
when it looks down upon itself!
Mourning it sees, then, misery and night and death!

But Thou callest me out of my night, Thou who succorest in
    misery and in death!
Then it comes over me that Thou createst me for eternity,
Noble One! for whom no praise, below in the grave, above at the
    throne,
Lord, Lord God! glowing with thanks, no rejoicing is sufficient.

Wave, trees of life, with the sound of the harp!
Roar with them in the sound of the harp, o crystal stream!
No matter how it murmurs and throbs, harps, your sound
is never enough! God it is whom ye praise!

Thunder, worlds, in your solemn course; in the chorus of
    trumpets,
thou, Orion, thou also, Libra!
Sound forth, all suns, in your shining row,
in the chorus of trumpets!

Ye worlds, thunder,
and you, chorus of trumpets, resound,
never enough, God, never enough, God,
God, God it is whom ye praise!

The Maiden's Lament

The oak forest roars, the clouds bluster,
the maiden sits on the green shore;

Es bricht sich die Welle mit Macht, mit Macht,
Und sie seufzet hinaus in die finstre Nacht,
Das Auge von Weinen getrübet.

"Das Herz ist gestorben, die Welt ist leer,
Und weiter gibt sie dem Wunsche nichts mehr.
Du Heilige, rufe dein Kind zurück,
Ich habe genossen das irdische Glück,
Ich habe gelebt und geliebet!"

Es rinnet der Träne vergeblicher Lauf,
Die Klage, sie wecket die Toten nicht auf;
Doch nenne, was tröstet und heilet die Brust
Nach der süssen Liebe verschwundener Lust,
Ich, die Himmlische, will's nicht versagen.

Lass rinnen der Tränen vergeblichen Lauf!
Es wecke die Klage den Toten nicht auf!
Das süsseste Glück für die trauernde Brust
Nach der schönen Liebe verschwundener Lust
Sind der Liebe Schmerzen und Klagen.

Friedrich von Schiller, 1759–1805

(Felix Mendelssohn-Bartholdy; others)

Der Doppelgänger, D. 957, no. 13

Still ist die Nacht, es ruhen die Gassen,
In diesem Hause wohnte mein Schatz;
Sie hat schon längst die Stadt verlassen,
Doch steht noch das Haus auf demselben Platz.

Da steht auch ein-Mensch und starrt in die Höhe,
Und ringt die Hände von Schmerzensgewalt;
Mir graut es, wenn ich sein Antlitz sehe—
Der Mond zeigt mir meine eigne Gestalt.

the waves break mightily, mightily,
and she sighs out into the gloomy night,
her eyes dimmed from weeping.

"My heart is dead, the world is empty,
and there is nothing more to wish for.
O Holy One, call your child back,
I have enjoyed the happiness of the earth,
I have lived and loved!"

Tears run their unavailing course,
laments don't awaken the dead;
but call, what cures and comforts the breast
after the lost happiness of sweet love,
I, the Holy One, will not refuse it.

Let the tears run their unavailing course!
Laments don't awaken the dead!
The sweetest fortune for the mourning breast
after the lost happiness of sweet love,
is the pain and lamenting of love.

My Double

Still is the night, the streets are asleep.
In this house my love once lived.
She left the city long ago,
yet the house still stands on the same spot.

Another man stands there looking up,
and wrings his hands in agony.
I shudder to see his face—
the moonlight shows me my own form.

Du Doppelgänger, du bleicher Geselle!
Was äffst du nach mein Liebeslleid,
Das mich gequält auf dieser Stelle
So manche Nacht, in alter Zeit?

Heinrich Heine, 1797–1856

(Bernhard Molique, op. 34; Thorvald Otterström)

Du bist die Ruh, D. 776

Du bist die Ruh,
Der Friede mild,
Die Sehnsucht du,
Und was sie stillt.

Ich weihe dir
Voll Lust und Schmerz
Zur Wohnung hier
Mein Aug und Herz.

Kehr ein bei mir
Und schließe du
Still hinter dir
Die Pforte zu.

Treib andern Schmerz
Aus dieser Brust!
Voll sei dies Herz
Von deiner Lust.

Dies Augenzelt,
Von deinem Glanz
Allein erhellt,
O füll es ganz!

Friedrich Rückert, 1788–1866

*Fanny Mendelssohn Henselt, op. 7, no. 4; Siegfried Karg-Elert,
op. 54, no. 2; many others)*

O my double, pale comrade!
Why do you ape my unhappy love
which tortured me upon this spot
so many nights in the olden time?

You Are Tranquility

You are tranquility,
gentle peace;
you are longing
and that which quiets it.

I dedicate to you,
full of joy and pain,
for dwelling here
my eyes and heart.

Come to me
and close
quietly behind you
the gates!

Drive other grief
from out this breast!
Let my heart be full
of your joy.

My vision
by your radiance
alone is brightened—
Oh fill it wholly.

Der Einsame, D. 800

Wann meine Grillen schwirren,
Bei Nacht, am spät erwärmten Herd,
Dann sitz ich mit vergnügtem Sinn
Vertraulich zu der Flamme hin,
So leicht, so unbeschwert.

Ein trautes, stilles Stündchen
Bleibt man noch gern am Feuer wach,
Man schürt, wenn sich die Lohe senkt,
Die Funken auf und sinnt und denkt:
Nun abermal ein Tag!

Was Liebes oder Leides
Sein Lauf für uns dahergebracht,
Es geht noch einmal durch den Sinn;
Allein das Böse wirft man hin,
Es störe nicht die Nacht.

Zu einem frohen Traume
Bereitet man gemach sich gut,
Wann sorgenlos ein holdes Bild
Mit sanfter Lust die Seele füllt,
Ergibt man sich der Ruh.

Oh, wie ich mir gefalle
In meiner stillen Ländlichkeit!
Was in dem Schwarm der lauten Welt
Das irre Herz gefesselt hält,
Gibt nicht Zufriedenheit.

Zirpt immer, liebe Heimchen,
In meiner Klause eng und klein.
Ich duld euch gern: ihr stört mich nicht,
Wenn euer Lied das Schweigen bricht,
Bin ich nicht ganz allein.

Carl Lappe, 1773–1843

The Solitary

When my crickets chirp
late at night by the warm hearth,
then I sit contentedly,
cosily by the fire,
so carefree, so at ease.

An intimate, silent little hour
I like to linger awake by the fire;
I poke the fire when it sinks;
the sparks fly up; I reflect and think,
another day gone by!

What happiness or sorrow
it has brought for us
passes again through my mind;
but I reject the bad things
so that they do not disturb the night.

For a happy dream
I prepare myself calmly.
When, without a care, a fond image
fills my soul with gentle joy
I give myself to rest.

O how contented I am
with my quiet country life!
Whatever in the crowding of the noisy world
holds the straying heart in shackles,
it does not give content.

Chirp on, dear crickets,
in my hermitage, narrow and small,
I bear with you gladly: you don't disturb me.
When your song breaks the silence
I am not altogether alone.

Erlkönig, D. 328

Wer reitet so spät durch Nacht und Wind?
Es ist der Vater mit seinem Kind;
Er hat den Knaben wohl in dem Arm,
Er fasst ihn sicher, er hält ihn warm.

Mein Sohn, was birgst du so bang dein Gesicht?—
Siehst, Vater, du den Erlkönig nicht?
Den Erlenkönig mit Kron' und Schweif?—
Mein Sohn, es ist ein Nebelstreif.—

"Du liebes Kind, komm, geh mit mir!
Gar schöne Spiele spiel' ich mit dir,
Manch bunte Blumen sind an dem Strand,
Meine Mutter hat manch gülden Gewand."

Mein Vater, mein Vater, und hörest du nicht,
Was Erlenkönig mir leise verspricht?—
Sei ruhig, bleibe ruhig, mein Kind:
In dürren Blättern säuselt der Wind.—

"Willst, feiner Knabe, du mit mir gehn?
Meine Töchter sollen dich warten schön;
Meine Töchter führen den nächtlichen Reihn
Und wiegen und tanzen und singen dich ein."

Mein Vater, mein Vater, und siehst du nicht dort
Erlkönigs Töchter am düstern Ort?—
Mein Sohn, mein Sohn, ich seh' es genau:
Es scheinen die alten Weiden so grau.—

"Ich liebe dich, mich reizt deine schöne Gestalt;
Und bist du nicht willig, so brauch' ich Gewalt."
Mein Vater, mein Vater, jetzt fasst er mich an!
Erlkönig hat mir ein Leids getan!—

The Erl-King

Who rides so late through night and wind?
It is the father with his child;
he folds the boy close in his arms,
he clasps him securely, he holds him warmly.

"My son, why do you hide your face so anxiously?"
"Father, don't you see the Erl-King?
The Erl-King with his crown and his train?"
"My son, it is a streak of mist."

"Dear child, come go with me!
I'll play the prettiest games with you.
Many colored flowers grow along the shore;
my mother has many golden garments."

"My father, my father, and don't you hear
the Erl-King whispering promises to me?"
"Be quiet, stay quiet, my child;
the wind is rustling in the dead leaves."

"My handsome boy, will you come with me?
My daughters shall wait upon you;
my daughters lead off in the dance every night,
and cradle and dance and sing you to sleep."

"My father, my father, and don't you see there
the Erl-King's daughters in the shadows?"
"My son, my son, I see it clearly;
the old willows look so gray."

"I love you, your beautiful figure delights me!
And if you are not willing, then I shall use force!"
"My father, my father, now he is taking hold of me!
The Erl-King has hurt me!"

Dem Vater grauset's, er reitet geschwind,
Er hält in Armen das ächzende Kind,
Erreicht den Hof mit Mühe und Not;
In seinen Armen das Kind war tot.

Johann Wolfgang von Goethe, 1749–1832

*(Carl Loewe, op. 1, no. 3; Johann Friedrich Reichardt; Louis
Spohr, op. 154, bk. 2, no. 4; others)*

Erster Verlust, D. 226

Ach, wer bringt die schönen Tage,
Jene Tage der ersten Liebe,
Ach, wer bringt nur eine Stunde
Jener holden Zeit zurück!

Einsam nähr ich meine Wunde,
Und mit stets erneuter Klage
Traur ich ums verlorne Glück.

Ach, wer bringt die schönen Tage,
Jene holde Zeit zurück!

Johann Wolfgang von Goethe, 1749–1832

*(Felix Mendelssohn-Bartholdy, op. 99, no. 1; Nicolai Medtner,
op. 6, no. 8; Othmar Schoeck, op. 15, no. 5; others)*

Der Fischer, D. 225

Das Wasser rauscht', das Wasser schwoll,
Ein Fischer saß daran,
Sah nach dem Angel ruhevoll,
Kühl bis ans Herz hinan.

The father shudders, he rides swiftly on;
he holds in his arms the groaning child.
He reaches the courtyard weary and anxious:
in his arms the child was dead.

First Loss

Ah, who will bring back the beautiful days,
the days of first love?
Ah, who will bring back only one hour
of that charming time?

Alone I nurse my wounds,
and with ever renewed complaints
I mourn for my lost happiness.

Ah, who will bring back the beautiful days,
that charming time?

The Fisherman

The water roared, the water swelled,
a fisherman sat nearby,
looked calmly at his line,
cool to his very heart.

Und wie er sitzt und wie er lauscht,
Teilt sich die Flut empor;
Aus dem bewegten Wasser rauscht
Ein feuchtes Weib hervor.

Sie sang zu ihm, sie sprach zu ihm:
Was lockst du meine Brut
Mit Menschenwitz und Menschenlist
Hinauf in Todesglut?
Ach wüßtest du, wie's Fischlein ist
So wohlig auf dem Grund,
Du stiegst herunter, wie du bist,
Und würdest erst gesund.

Labt sich die liebe Sonne nicht,
Der Mond sich nicht im Meer?
Kehrt wellenatmend ihr Gesicht
Nicht doppelt schöner her?
Lockt dich der tiefe Himmel nicht,
Das feuchtverklärte Blau?
Lockt dich dein eigen Angesicht
Nicht her in ewgen Tau?

Das Wasser rauscht', das Wasser schwoll,
Netzt' ihm den nackten Fuß;
Sein Herz wuchs ihm so sehnsuchtsvoll,
Wie bei ber Liebsten Gruß.
Sie sprach zu ihm, sie sang zu ihm;
Da wars um ihn geschehn:
Halb zog sie ihn, halb sank er hin,
Und ward nicht mehr gesehn.

Johann Wolfgang von Goethe, 1749–1832

(Johann Friedrich Reichardt; Carl Friedrich Zelter; Carl Loewe,
op. 43, no. 1; Hugo Wolf; others)

And as he sat and as he listened
the river surged upward,
and from the moving water burst up
a mermaid.

She sang to him, she spoke to him,
why do you tempt my brood,
with man's wit and man's guile,
up to a glowing death?
Ah, if you knew how it is for the little fish,
so very pleasant,
you would come down as you are
and for the first time be well.

Doesn't the sun refresh itself,
and the moon, in the sea?
Do they not return, breathing waves,
with their faces twice as beautiful?
Doesn't the moist radiance of heaven
draw you?
Doesn't your own face draw you,
here in eternal dew?

The water roared, the water swelled,
wetting his bare foot;
his heart grew so full of longing,
as at the greeting of love.
She spoke to him, she sang to him,
for him that was the end.
She half pulled him, half sank him,
and he was never seen again.

Die Forelle, D. 550

In einem Bächlein helle,
Da schoß in froher Eil
Die launische Forelle
Vorüber wie ein Pfeil.
Ich stand an dem Gestade
Und sah in süßer Ruh
Des muntern Fischleins Bade
Im klaren Bächlein zu.

Ein Fischer mit der Rute
Wohl an dem Ufer stand,
Und sah's mit kaltem Blute,
Wie sich das Fischlein wand.
So lang dem Wasser Helle,
So dacht ich, nicht gebricht,
So fängt er die Forelle
Mit seiner Angel nicht.

Doch endlich ward dem Diebe
Die Zeit zu lang.
Er macht das Bächlein tückisch trübe,
Und eh ich es gedacht,
So zuckte seine Rute,
Das Fischlein zappelt dran,
Und ich mit regem Blute
Sah die Betrogene an.

Christian Daniel Schubart, 1739–91

Frühlingsglaube, D. 686

Die linden Lüfte sind erwacht,
Sie säuseln und weben Tag und Nacht,

The Trout

In a clear brooklet,
with happy haste,
a playful trout
darted about like an arrow.
I stood on the bank
and contentedly watched
the merry fish bathe
in the clear brooklet.

A fisherman with his rod
stood on the bank
and looked on heartlessly
as the fish wriggled about.
So long as the clear water—
I thought—is not disturbed,
he will not catch the trout
with his hook.

But suddenly the thief
got tired of waiting. He
slyly muddied the brook,
and before I realized it
he jerked his rod
and the fish struggled on the line.
And I, with my pulse beating high,
watched the victim.

Faith in Spring

The soft winds have awakened,
they sough and stir day and night;

Sie schaffen an allen Enden.
O frischer Duft, o neuer Klang!
Nun, armes Herze, sei nicht bang!
Nun muß sich alles, alles wenden.

Die Welt wird schöner mit jedem Tag,
Man weiß nicht, was noch werden mag,
Das Blühen will nicht enden;
Es blüht das fernste, tiefste Tal:
Nun, armes Herz, vergiß der Qual!
Nun muß sich alles, alles wenden.

Johann Ludwig Uhland, 1787–1862

*(Felix Mendelssohn-Bartholdy, op. 9, no. 8; Louis Spohr, op. 72,
no. 13; Karl Friedrich Curschmann; others)*

Geheimes, D. 719

Über meines Liebchens Äugelein
Stehn verwundert alle Leute;
Ich, der Wissende, dagegen,
Weiß recht gut, was das bedeute.

Denn es heißt: Ich liebe diesen,
Und nicht etwa den und jenen.
Lasset nur, ihr guten Leute,
Euer Wundern, euer Sehnen!

Ja, mit ungeheuren Mächten
Blicket sie wohl in die Runde;
Doch sie sucht nur zu verkünden
Ihm die nächste süße Stunde.

Johann Wolfgang von Goethe, 1749–1832

(Wenzel Johann Tomaschek, op. 58)

they bring life on all sides.
O fresh fragrance! O new sounds!
Now, poor heart, don't be anxious,
now must everything change.

The world grows more beautiful with every day;
one doesn't know what still may happen—
the blooming will not end.
It blooms in the farthest, deepest valley.
Now, poor heart, forget the torment!
Now must everything change.

Secret

My beloved's eyes
astonish everyone;
I, the authority on the subject,
know very well what this means.

For she is saying: I love this one,
and not at all that one or the other.
Leave off, good people,
your wondering and your desire.

Yes, with uncanny powers
she looks around her;
yet she only means to announce
to him the next sweet hour.

Gretchen am Spinnrade, D. 118

Meine Ruh ist hin,
Mein Herz ist schwer,
Ich finde sie nimmer
Und nimmermehr.

Wo ich ihn nicht hab,
Ist mir das Grab,
Die ganze Welt
Ist mir vergällt.

Mein armer Kopf
Ist mir verrückt,
Mein armer Sinn
ist mir zerstückt.

Meine Ruh ist hin,
Mein Herz ist schwer,
Ich finde sie nimmer
und nimmermehr.

Nach ihm nur schau ich
Zum Fenster hinaus,
Nach ihm nur geh ich
Aus dem Haus.

Sein hoher Gang,
Sein' edle Gestalt,
Seines Mundes Lächeln,
Seiner Augen Gewalt,

Und seiner Rede
Zauberfluss,
Sein Händedruck,
Und ach, sein Kuss!

Gretchen at the Spinning Wheel

My peace is gone,
my heart is heavy;
I shall never find it,
never again.

Where I do not have him
it is like the grave to me,
the whole world
is bitter.

My poor head
is deranged,
my poor mind
is distracted.

My peace is gone,
my heart is heavy;
I shall never find it,
never again.

Only for him
I look out of the window;
only for him I
leave the house.

His fine bearing,
his noble form,
the smile of his lips,
the power of his eyes,

and the magic flow
of his talk,
the clasp of his hands,
and ah, his kiss!

Meine Ruh ist hin,
Mein Herz ist schwer,
Ich finde sie nimmer
Und nimmermehr.

Mein Busen drängt
Sich nach ihm hin.
Ach dürft' ich fassen
Und halten ihn,

Und küssen ihn,
So wie ich wollt,
An seinen Küssen
Vergehen sollt!

Johann Wolfgang von Goethe, 1749–1832

(Carl Loewe, op. 9; Louis Spohr, op. 25, no. 3; Conradin Kreutzer; Carl Friedrich Curschmann, op. 11, no. 5)

Gruppe aus dem Tartarus, D. 583

Horch—wie Murmeln des empörten Meeres, Wie durch hohler
  Felsen Becken weint ein Bach,
Stöhnt dort dumpfigtief ein schweres, leeres Qualerpresstes Ach!

Schmerz verzerret
Ihr Gesicht; Verzweiflung sperret Ihren Rachen fluchend auf.
Hohl sind ihre Augen, ihre Blicke Spähen bang nach des Cocytus
  Brücke, Folgen tränend seinem Trauerlauf,

Fragen sich einander ängstlichleise, Ob noch nicht Vollendung
  sei?—
Ewigkeit schwingt über ihnen Kreise, Bricht die Sense des Saturns
  entzwei.

Friedrich von Schiller, 1759–1805

(Fartein Valen, op. 31, no. 1)

My peace is gone,
my heart is heavy;
I shall never find it,
never again.

My bosom yearns
for him;
ah, could I grasp him
and hold him

and kiss him
to my heart's content,
under his kisses
to swoon!

Group in Tartarus

Hark—like the murmur of the swelling sea,
as if through its hollowed, rocky basin, a brook is weeping,
there sounds, damp and deep, a heavy, empty,
tormented cry!

Pain distorts
their faces; despair sets
their cursing jaws agape.
Empty are their eyes, their glances
peer fearfully toward the bridge of Cocytus;
weeping they follow its doleful course.

They ask each other anxiously and softly
whether there is never an end?—
Eternity swings circles over them,
and breaks the scythe of Saturn in two.

Heidenröslein, D. 257

Sah ein Knab' ein Röslein stehn,
Röslein auf der Heiden,
War so jung und morgenschön,
Lief er schnell, es nah zu sehn,
Sah's mit vielen Freuden.
Röslein, Röslein, Röslein rot,
Röslein auf der Heiden.

Knabe sprach: "Ich breche dich,
Röslein auf der Heiden!"
Röslein sprach: "Ich steche dich,
Dass du ewig denkst an mich,
Und ich will's nicht leiden."
Röslein, Röslein, Röslein rot,
Röslein auf der Heiden.

Und der wilde Knabe brach
's Röslein auf der Heiden;
Röslein wehrte sich und stach,
Half ihm doch kein Weh und Ach,
Musst' es eben leiden.
Röslein, Röslein, Röslein rot,
Röslein auf der Heiden.

Johann Wolfgang von Goethe, 1749–1832

*(Heinrich Werner, 1827; Johann Friedrich Reichardt; Carl
Gottlieb Reissiger, op. 79, no. 3; Wilhelm Taubert, op. 5, no. 2)*

Der Hirt auf dem Felsen, D. 965

Wenn auf dem höchsten Fels ich steh,
Ins tiefe Tal herniederseh,
Und singe:

The Wild Rosebud

A lad saw a rosebud,
rosebud on the heath;
it was so young in its morning beauty
that he ran to look at it more closely.
He gazed at it with great pleasure.
Rosebud red,
rosebud on the heath.

The lad said: "I'll pick you,
rosebud on the heath!"
The rosebud said: "I'll prick you,
so that you will always think of me,
and I will not stand for it."
Rosebud red,
rosebud on the heath.

And the brutal lad picked
the rosebud on the heath;
the rosebud defended itself and pricked,
yet no grief and lamentation helped it:
it simply had to suffer.
Rosebud red,
rosebud on the heath.

The Shepherd on the Rock

When I stand on the highest rock,
gaze down deep into the valley
and sing:

Fern aus dem tiefen dunklen Tal
Schwingt sich empor der Widerhall
Der Klüfte.

Je weiter meine Stimme dringt,
Je heller sie mir widerklingt
Von unten.
Mein Liebchen wohnt so weit von mir,
Drum sehn ich mich so heiss nach ihr
Hinüber.

Im tiefem Gram verzehr ich mich,
Mir ist die Friede hin,
Auf Erden mir die Hoffnung wich,
Ich hier so einsam bin.

So sehnend klang im Wald das Lied,
So sehnend klang es durch die Nacht,
Die Herzen es zum Himmel zieht
Mit wunderbarer Macht.
Der Frühling will kommen,
Der Frühling mein Freund,
Nun mach ich mich fertig
Zum Wandern bereit.

Je weiter meine Stimme dringt,
Je heller sie mir widerklingt
Von unten.

Wilhelm Müller, 1794–1828 and Helmine von Chezy, 1783–1856

Im Abendrot, D. 799

O wie schön ist deine Welt,
Vater, wenn sie golden strahlet!
Wenn dein Glanz herniederfällt,

from far in the deep, dark valley
arises an echo
of the caves.

The farther my voice carries
the clearer its echo
from below.
My sweetheart lives so far from here,
that I long passionately for her
over there.

I am consumed with deep grief;
my happiness is gone,
my hope on earth is gone,
I am so lonely here.

So longingly my song sounded in the wood,
so longingly it sounded through the night,
that it drew hearts to heaven
with wonderful power.
Spring is coming,
spring, my friend.
Now I am making ready,
ready to wander.

The farther my voice carries,
the clearer its echo
from below.

In the Evening Glow

O how beautiful is Thy world,
Father, when it shines like gold;
when Thy radiance descends

Und den Staub mit Schimmer malet,
Wenn das Rot, das in der Wolke blinkt,
In mein stilles Fenster sinkt!

Könnt ich klagen, könnt ich zagen?
Irre sein an dir und mir?
Nein, ich will im Busen tragen
Deinen Himmel schon allhier.
Und dies Herz, eh es zusammenbricht,
Trinkt noch Glut und schlürft noch Licht.

Karl Lappe, 1773–1843

Im Frühling, D. 882

Still sitz ich an des Hügels Hang,
Der Himmel ist so klar,
Das Lüftchen spielt im grünen Tal,
Wo ich beim ersten Frühlingsstrahl
Einst, ach so glücklich war.
Wo ich an ihrer Seite ging
So traulich und so nah,
und tief im dunklen Felsenquell
Den schönen Himmel blau und hell
Und sie im Himmel sah.

Sieh, wie der bunte Frühling schon
Aus Knosp und Blüte blickt!
Nicht alle Blüten sind mir gleich,
Am liebsten pflück ich von dem Zweig,
Von welchem sie gepflückt!
Denn alles ist wie damals noch,
Die Blumen, das Gefild;
Die Sonne scheint nicht minder hell,
Nicht minder freundlich schwimmt im Quell
Das blaue Himmelsbild.

and paints the dust with splendor;
when the red that gleams in the clouds
falls upon my silent window.

Could I complain? Could I waver?
Doubt Thee and myself?
No, I will carry in my breast
Thy heaven even here;
and this heart, ere it fails,
shall still drink in the warmth and relish the light.

In Spring

Quietly I sit on the side of the hill;
the sky is so clear.
The breeze plays in the green valley
where I, in the first light of spring,
once was so happy!
Where I walked at her side,
so intimate and so close,
and deep in the dark rock-spring
saw the beautiful heaven, blue and bright,
and saw her in that heaven.

See how the colorful spring already
looks out of the buds and blossoms!
Not all the flowers are the same to me,
I like best to pick from the branch
from which she picked!
For all is as it used to be,
the flowers, the fields;
the sun shines no less brightly,
no less cheerfully floats in the spring
the blue image of heaven.

Es wandeln nur sich Will und Wahn,
Es wechseln Lust und Streit,
Vorüber flieht der Liebe Glück,
Und nur die Liebe bleibt zurück,
Die Lieb und ach, das Leid.
O wär ich doch ein Vöglein Nur
Dort an dem Wiesenhang,
Dann blieb ich auf den Zweigen hier,
Und säng ein süßes Lied von ihr,
Den ganzen Sommer lang.

Ernst Konrad Friedrich Schulze, 1789–1817

Der Jüngling an der Quelle, D. 300

Leise, rieselnder Quell!
Ihr wallenden, flispernden Pappeln!
Euer Schlummergeräusch
Wecket die Liebe nur auf.
Linderung sucht ich bei euch,
Und sie zu vergessen, die Spröde, ach,
Und Blätter und Bach
Seufzen, Luise, dir nach.

Johann Gaudene, Freiherr von Salis-Sewis, 1763–1834

Die junge Nonne, D. 825

Wie braust durch die Wipfel der heulende Sturm!
Es klirren die Balken, es zittert das Haus!
Es rollet der Donner, es leuchtet der Blitz,
Und finster die Nacht wie das Grab!

Immerhin, immerhin,
So tobt es auch jüngst noch in mir!

Only the will and the fancy change,
pleasure turns to strife;
the happiness of love flees away,
and only love remains behind—
love, and alas, sorrow!
Oh, if I were only a bird
there on the hillside meadow,
then I would stay in the branches here
and sing a sweet song about her
all summer long.

The Youth at the Spring

Quiet, purling spring!
And you, rustling, whispering poplars!
Your drowsy stirring
only awakens love.
I came to you for consolation,
and to forget my coy mistress, ah,
and the leaves and the brook
sigh "Louise" around you.

The Young Nun

How the raging storm howls through the treetops!
The rafters rattle, the house trembles!
The thunder rolls, the lightning flashes,
and the night is gloomy as the grave!

Ever so, ever so,
not long ago it raged within me!

Es brauste das Leben, wie jetzo der Sturm,
Es bebte die Glieder, wie jetzo das Haus.
Es flammte die Liebe, wie jetzo der Blitz,
Und finster die Brust wie das Grab.

Nun tobe, du wilder, gewaltiger Sturm,
Im Herzen ist Friede, im Herzen ist Ruh;
Des Bräutigams harret die liebende Braut,
Gereinigt in prüfender Glut,
Der ewigen Liebe getraut.

Ich harre, mein Heiland! mit sehnendem Blick!
Komm, himmlischer Bräutigam, hole die Braut,
Erlöse die Seele von irdischer Haft!
Horch, friedlich ertönet das Glöcklein vom Turm!
Es lockt mich das süsse Getön
Allmächtig zu ewigen Höhn.
Alleluja! Alleluja!

Jakob Nikolaus, Reichsherr von Craigher de Jachelutta,
1797–1855

Lachen und Weinen, D. 777

Lachen und Weinen zu jeglicher Stunde
Ruht bei der Lieb auf so mancherlei Grunde.
Morgens lacht ich vor Lust,
Und warum ich nun weine
Bei des Abendes Scheine,
Ist mir selb' nicht bewußt.

Weinen und Lachen zu jeglicher Stunde
Ruht bei der Lieb auf so mancherlei Grunde.
Abends weint ich vor Schmerz;
Und warum du erwachen kannst
Am Morgen mit Lachen,
Muß ich dich fragen, o Herz.

Friedrich Rückert, 1788–1866

Life blustered as now the storm;
my limbs shivered as now the house;
love flamed as now the lightning,
and my heart was gloomy as the grave!

Now rage, wild mighty storm:
in my heart there is peace, in my heart there is rest.
The loving bride awaits the bridegroom,
cleansed by the proving fire,
pledged to eternal love.

I wait, my Savior, with longing eyes!
Come, Heavenly Bridegroom, come for the bride;
release the soul from earthly ties!
Hark! Peacefully the bell rings from the tower!
The sweet sound calls me
irresistibly to the eternal heights.
Alleluia!

Laughter and Crying

Laughter and crying, at different hours
have such different reasons, when one is in love.
In the morning I laugh for joy;
and why do I cry now
in the evening light?
I myself don't know.

Crying and laughter, at different hours
have such different reasons, when one is in love.
In the evening I cried for grief;
then how can you wake up
laughing in the morning?—
I must ask you, my heart.

Der Leiermann, D. 911, no. 24

Drüben hinterm Dorfe
Steht ein Leiermann,
Und mit starren Fingern
Dreht er, was er kann.

Barfuß auf dem Eise
Wankt er hin und her,
Und sein kleiner Teller
Bleibt ihm immer leer.

Keiner mag ihn hören,
Keiner sieht ihn an,
Und die Hunde knurren
Um den alten Mann.

Und er läßt es gehen
Alles, wie es will,
Dreht, und seine Leier
Steht ihm nimmer still.

Wunderlicher Alter!
Soll ich mit dir gehn?
Willst zu meinen Liedern
Deine Leier drehn?

Wilhelm Müller, 1794–1827

Die Liebe hat gelogen, D. 751

Die Liebe hat gelogen,
Die Sorge lastet schwer,
Betrogen, ach! betrogen
Hat alles mich umher!

The Hurdy-Gurdy Man

Over beyond the village
stands a hurdy-gurdy man,
and with his numb fingers
he grinds as best he can.

Barefoot on the ice
he moves to and fro,
and his little tray
remains always empty.

Nobody cares to hear him,
nobody looks at him;
and the dogs snarl
around the old man.

And he lets everything go
as it will;
he grinds, and his hurdy-gurdy
is never silent.

Queer old man,
shall I go with you?
Will you grind out my songs
on your hurdy-gurdy?

Love Has Been Lying

Love has been lying,
grief presses heavily;
betrayed, ah betrayed
by everything around me!

Es fließen heiße Tropfen
Die Wange stets herab,
Laß ab, mein Herz, zu klopfen,
Du armes Herz, laß ab!

Die Liebe hat gelogen,
Die Sorge lastet schwer,
Betrogen, ach! betrogen
Hat alles mich umher!

August von Platen, 1796–1835

Liebhaber in allen Gestalten, D. 558

Ich wollt, ich wär ein Fisch,
So hurtig und frisch;
Und kämst du zu angeln,
Ich würde nicht mangeln.
Ich wollt, ich wär ein Fisch,
So hurtig und frisch.

Ich wollt, ich wäre Gold,
Dir immer im Sold;
Und tätst du was kaufen,
Käm ich wieder gelaufen.
Ich wollt, ich wäre Gold,
Dir immer im Sold.

Doch bin ich, wie ich bin,
Und nimm mich nur hin!
Willst du beßre besitzen,
So laß dir sie schnitzen.
Ich bin nur, wie ich bin;
So nimm mich nur hin!

Johann Wolfgang von Goethe, 1749–1832

Warm drops flow
ever down my cheeks;
stop beating, my heart,
poor heart, stop!

Love has been lying,
grief presses heavily;
betrayed, ah betrayed
by everything around me!

The Lover in All Shapes

I wish I were a fish,
so agile and lively;
if you were to come angling
I wouldn't fail you.
I wish I were a fish,
so agile and lively.

I wish I were gold,
always at your service,
and if you wanted to buy something
I would come running back to you.
I wish I were gold,
always at your service.

But I am what I am,
so just take me!
If you want better lovers,
have them custom-carved for you.
I am only what I am,
so just take me.

Lied eines Schiffers an die Dioskuren, D. 360

Dioskuren, Zwillingssterne,
Die ihr leuchtet meinem Nachen,
Mich beruhigt auf dem Meere
Eure Milde, euer Wachen.

Wer auch fest in sich begründet,
Unverzagt dem Sturm begegnet,
Fühlt sich doch in euren Strahlen
Doppelt mutig und gesegnet.

Dieses Ruder, das ich schwinge,
Meeresfluten zu zerteilen,
Hänge ich, so ich geborgen,
Auf an eures Tempels Säulen,
Dioskuren, Zwillingssterne.

Johann Mayrhofer, 1787–1836

Der Lindenbaum, D. 911, no. 5

Am Brunnen vor dem Tore,
Da steht ein Lindenbaum;
Ich träumt in seinem Schatten
So manchen süßen Traum.

Ich schnitt in seine Rinde
So manches liebe Wort;
Es zog in Freud und Leide
Zu ihm mich immer fort.

Ich mußt auch heute wandern
Vorbei in tiefer Nacht,
Da hab ich noch im Dunkeln
Die Augen zugemacht.

Song of a Boatman to the Dioscuri

Dioscuri, twin stars
who light my boat,
I am calmed on the sea
by your gentleness, under your care.

He too who is confident in himself
stands resolutely against the storm,
yet feels himself in your light
doubly brave and blessed.

This oar that I ply
to plough the waves of the sea,
I hang when I am safe
on the pillars of your temple,
Dioscuri, twin stars.

The Linden Tree

By the well in front of the gate
there stands a linden tree;
I have dreamed in its shade
many a sweet dream.

I have carved in its bark
many a fond word;
in joy and in sorrow
I have always felt drawn to it.

I had to pass it again just now
in the deep night,
and even in the dark
I closed my eyes.

Und seine Zweige rauschten,
Als riefen sie mir zu:
Komm her zu mir, Geselle,
Hier findst du deine Ruh!

Die kalten Winde bliesen
Mir grad ins Angesicht,
Der Hut flog mir vom Kopfe,
Ich wendete mich nicht.

Nun bin ich manche Stunde
Entfernt von diesem Ort,
Und immer hör ich's rauschen:
Du fändest Ruhe dort!

Wilhelm Müller, 1794–1827

(Ludwig Erk)

Der Musensohn, D. 764

Durch Feld und Wald zu schweifen,
Mein Liedchen weg zu pfeifen,
So geht's von Ort zu Ort!
Und nach dem Takte reget
Und nach dem Maß beweget
Sich alles an mir fort.

Ich kann sie kaum erwarten,
Die erste Blum im Garten,
Die erste Blüt am Baum.
Sie grüßen meine Lieder,
Und kommt der Winter wieder,
Sing ich noch jenen Traum.

Ich sing ihn in der Weite,
Auf Eises Läng und Breite,

And its branches rustled,
as if they were calling to me:
"Come here, friend,
here you will find rest!"

The cold winds blew
right into my face;
my hat flew off my head,
yet I did not turn back.

Now I am many hours
distant from that spot,
yet I always hear it rustling:
"you would find rest there!"

The Poet

To ramble through field and forest,
to pipe away my little song,
so it goes from place to place!
and to my beat
and to my measure
everything moves.

I can hardly wait
for the first flower in the garden,
the first bloom on the tree.
They greet my songs,
and when winter comes again
I am still singing of that dream.

I sing it far and wide
over the length and breadth of ice,

Da blüht der Winter schön!
Auch diese Blüte schwindet,
Und neue Freude findet
Sich auf bebauten Höhn.

Denn wie ich bei der Linde
Das junge Völkchen finde,
Sogleich erreg ich sie.
Der stumpfe Bursche bläht sich,
Das steife Mädchen dreht sich
Nach meiner Melodie.

Ihr gebt den Sohlen Flügel
Und treibt durch Tal und Hügel
Den Liebling weit vom Haus.
Ihr lieben, holden Musen,
Wann ruh ich ihr am Busen
Auch endlich wieder aus?

Johann Wolfgang von Goethe, 1749–1832

(Johann Friedrich Reichardt; Carl Friedrich Zelter)

Nacht und Träume, D. 827

Heilge Nacht, du sinkest nieder;
Nieder wallen auch die Träume,
Wie dein Mondlicht durch die Räume,
Durch der Menschen stille Brust.
Die belauschen sie mit Lust;
Rufen, wenn der Tag erwacht:
Kehre wieder, heilge Nacht!
Holde Träume, kehret wieder!

Matthäus von Collin, 1779–1824

and winter blossoms beautifully!
These flowers also vanish,
and new happiness is found
in the upland farms.

For when under the linden
I find the young people,
at once I excite them.
The dull boy struts,
the stiff girl turns
to my melody.

You give wings to my feet
and drive over vale and hill
your loved one, far from home.
O dear, gentle muses,
when shall I rest again upon your bosom
at last?

Night and Dreams

Hallowed night, you are descending;
dreams, too, come drifting down—
like your moonlight through space—
delightfully through the hearts of men.

They listen to her with joy;
they call out when day breaks:
Come back, hallowed night!
Gracious dreams, come back again.

Nähe des Geliebten, D. 162

Ich denke dein, wenn mir der Sonne Schimmer
Vom Meere strahlt;
Ich denke dein, wenn sich des Mondes Flimmer
In Quellen malt.

Ich sehe dich, wenn auf dem fernen Wege
Der Staub sich hebt;
In tiefer Nacht, wenn auf dem schmalen Stege
Der Wandrer bebt.

Ich höre dich, wenn dort mit dumpfem Rauschen
Die Welle steigt.
Im stillen Hain, da geh ich oft zu lauschen,
Wenn alles schweigt.

Ich bin bei dir; du seist such noch so ferne,
Du bist mir nah!
Die Sonne sinkt, bald leuchten mir die Sterne,
O wärst du da!

Johann Wolfgang von Goethe, 1749–1832

*(Ludwig van Beethoven, WoO 74; Carl Loewe, op. 9, Heft III,
no. 1; Eduard Lassen, op. 62, no. 1; many others)*

Der Neugierige, D. 795, no. 6

Ich frage keine Blume,
Ich frage keinen Stern;
Sie können mir alle nicht sagen,
Was ich erführ so gern.

Ich bin ja auch kein Gärtner,
Die Sterne stehn zu hoch;

Near to the Beloved

I think of you when the shimmer of the sun
shines on the sea;
I think of you when the glimmer of the moon
is pictured in the springs.

I see you when on the distant way
the dust rises;
in the deep night, when on the narrow path
the traveler quakes.

I hear you when with dull roar
the wave swells up.
In the quiet grove I often go to listen
when all is still.

I am with you, however far away you may be,
you are with me!
The sun sets, soon the stars shine on me.
o that you were here!

The Questioner

I do not ask a flower,
I do not ask a star;
they all could not tell me
what I want so much to know.

Anyway, I am no gardner;
the stars are too high.

Mein Bächlein will ich fragen,
Ob mich mein Herz belog.

O Bächlein meiner Liebe,
Wie bist du heut so stumm!
Will ja nur eines wissen,
Ein Wörtchen um und um.

"Ja" heißt das eine Wörtchen,
Das andre heißet "nein,"
Die beiden Wörtchen schließen
Die ganze Welt mir ein.

O Bächlein meiner Liebe,
Was bist du wunderlich!
Will's ja nicht weiter sagen,
Sag, Bächlein, liebt sie mich?

Wilhelm Müller, 1794–1827

Die Post, D. 911, no. 13

Von der Straße her ein Posthorn klingt.
Was hat es, daß es so hoch aufspringt,
Mein Herz?

Die Post bringt keinen Brief für dich.
Was drängst du denn so wunderlich,
Mein Herz?

Nun ja, die Post kommt aus der Stadt,
Wo ich ein liebes Liebchen hatt,
Mein Herz!

Willst wohl einmal hinübersehn
Und fragen, wie es dort mag gehn,
Mein Herz?

Wilhelm Müller, 1794–1827

I will ask the brooklet
if my heart is deceiving me.

O dear brooklet,
how quiet you are today!
I want to know only one thing,
one little word, over and over.

"Yes" is that one little word—
the other one is "No."
In these two words
the whole world is bound up for me.

O dear brooklet,
how strangely you behave!
I will not repeat what you say—
tell me, brooklet, does she love me?

The Mail Coach

Along the street a post-horn sounds.
What is it that makes you so excited,
my heart?

The mail coach brings no letter for you:
why, then, are you so strangely vexed,
my heart?

Oh, perhaps the coach comes from the town
where I had a sweetheart,
my heart!

Would you like to have a look over there,
and ask how things are going,
my heart?

Rastlose Liebe, D. 138

Dem Schnee, dem Regen,
Dem Wind entgegen,
Im Dampf der Klüfte,
Durch Nebeldüfte,
Immer zu! Immer zu!
Ohne Rast und Ruh!

Lieber durch Leiden
Möcht' ich mich schlagen,
Als so viel Freuden
Des Lebens ertragen.
Alle das Neigen
Von Herzen zu Herzen,
Ach, wie so eigen
Schaffet das Schmerzen!

Wie, soll ich fliehen?
Waldwärts ziehen?
Alles vergebens!
Krone des Lebens,
Glück ohne Ruh,
Liebe, bist du!

Johann Wolfgang von Goethe, 1749–1832

*(Robert Franz, op. 33, no. 6; Johann Friedrich Reichardt; Othmar
Schoeck; Joachim Raff, op. 98, no. 2; many others)*

Das Rosenband, D. 280

Im Frühlingsschatten fand ich sie,
Da band ich sie mit Rosenbändern:
Sie fühlt' es nicht und schlummerte.

Restless Love

Against the snow, the rain,
the wind,
in the midst of the ravines,
through the fragrant mists,
ever on! Ever on!
without rest or repose.

Rather would I struggle
through suffering
than to bear so much
of the world's joy.
All the inclining
of heart to heart,
ah, how in its own way
it causes pain!

What, shall I run away?
Flee to the woods?
All in vain!
Crown of life,
bliss without rest,
that is love!

The Rosy Ribbon

In the shadows of spring I found her;
I bound her with rosy ribbons.
She didn't feel it and was asleep.

Ich sah sie an; mein Leben hing
Mit diesem Blick an ihrem Leben:
Ich fühlte es wohl und wußt es nicht.

Doch lispelt ich ihr sprachlos zu
Und rauschte mit den Rosenbändern:
Da wachte sie vom Schlummer auf.

Sie sah mich an; ihr Leben hing
Mit diesem Blick an meinem Leben
Und um uns ward's Elysium.

Friedrich Gottlieb Klopstock, 1724–1803

(Richard Strauss, op. 36, no. 1; Carl Friedrich Zelter; others)

Sei mir gegrüßt!, D. 741

O du Entrißne mir und meinem Kusse,
Sei mir gegrüßt, sei mir geküßt!
Erreichbar nur meinem Sehnsuchtsgruße,
Sei mir gegrüßt, sei mir geküßt!

Du von der Hand der Liebe diesem Herzen Gegebne,
Du, von dieser Brust Genommne mir!
Mit diesem Tränengusse
Sei mir gegrüßt, sei mir geküßt!

Zum Trotz der Ferne, die sich feindlich trennend
Hat zwischen mich und dich gestellt;
Dem Neid der Schicksalsmächte zum Verdrusse
Sei mir gegrüßt, sei mir geküßt!

Wie du mir je im schönsten Lenz der Liebe
Mit Gruß und Kuß entgegenkamst,
Mit meiner Seele glühendstem Ergusse,
Sei mir gegrüßt, sei mir geküßt!

I looked at her; my life hung
with this look upon her life:
I felt it surely and did not know.

Yet I whispered to her voicelessly
and rustled the rosy ribbons.
Then she awoke from her sleep.

She looked at me; her life hung
with this look upon my life,
and around us became Elysium.

My Greeting to You!

O you, torn from me and my kiss,
I greet you, I kiss you!
To be reached only by my longing greeting,
I greet you, I kiss you!

You, given to this heart
by the hand of love; you, taken away
from this breast! With this gush of tears,
I greet you, I kiss you!

Despite the distance, hostile and divisive,
that has come between me and you;
to aggravate the envy of the powers of fate,
I greet you, I kiss you!

As you in the beautiful spring of love
came to me with a greeting and a kiss,
with my soul's ardent outpouring,
I greet you, I kiss you!

Ein Hauch der Liebe tilget Raum und Zeiten,
Ich bin bei dir, du bist bei mir,
Ich halte dich in dieses Arms Umschlusse,
Sei mir gegrüßt, sei mir geküßt!

Friedrich Rückert, 1788–1866

Seligkeit, D. 433

Freuden sonder Zahl
Blühn im Himmelssaal!
Engeln und Verklärten,
Wie die Väter lehrten.
O da möcht ich sein
Und mich ewig freun!

Jedem lächelt traut
Eine Himmelsbraut;
Harf und Psalter klinget,
Und man tanzt und singet.
O da möcht ich sein
Und mich ewig freun!

Lieber bleib ich hier,
Lächelt Laura mir
Einen Blick, der saget,
Daß ich ausgeklaget.
Selig dann mit ihr,
Bleib ich ewig hier!

Ludwig Heinrich Christoph Hölty, 1748–76

A breath of love obliterates space and time;
I am with you, you are with me,
I hold you in these arms' embrace,
I greet you, I kiss you!

Blessedness

Numberless joys
bloom in the hall of heaven!
For angels and transfigured ones,
as the fathers taught.
O, there I'd like to be
and rejoice forever!

On each one smiles lovingly
a heavenly bride;
harp and psaltery sound
and everyone dances and sings.
O there I'd like to be
and rejoice forever!

Rather I'll remain here
if Laura smiles at me
with a look that says
I am through with complaining.
Blessed then with her
I'll remain here forever.

Ständchen, D. 957, no. 4

Leise flehen meine Lieder
Durch die Nacht zu dir;
In den stillen Hain hernieder,
Liebchen, komm zu mir!

Flüsternd schlanke Wipfel rauschen
In des Mondes Licht,
Des Verräters feindlich Lauschen
Fürchte, Holde, nicht.

Hörst die Nachtigallen schlagen?
Ach! sie flehen dich,
Mit der Töne süßen Klagen
Flehen sie für mich.

Sie verstehn des Busens Sehnen,
Kennen Liebesschmerz,
Rühren mit den Silbertönen
Jedes weiche Herz.

Laß auch dir die Brust bewegen
Liebchen, höre mich,
Bebend harr ich dir entgegen!
Komm, beglücke mich!

Ludwig Rellstab, 1799–1860

*(Franz Lachner, op. 49, no. 6; C. Arnold, op. 14, no. 4; R.
Hertzberg, op. 3, no. 2)*

Der Tod und das Mädchen, D. 531

Das Mädchen: Vorüber, ach, vorüber! geh, wilder
Knochenmann!

Serenade

Softly pleading, my songs go
through the night to you;
in the quiet grove down here,
dearest, come to me!

Whispering tall treetops rustle
in the moonlight.
If treacherous ears may listen
do not fear, my dear.

Do you hear the nightingales' song?
Ah! they implore you,
with the sweet complaint of their music
they plead for me.

They understand the longing of my heart,
know the pain of love;
they touch with their silvery voices
every tender heart.

Let your heart, too, be moved—
dearest, hear me!
Trembling I await you!
Come and make me happy!

Death and the Maiden

The Maiden: Pass by, pass by, go, horrible skeleton!

Ich bin noch jung, geh, Lieber!
Und rühre mich nicht an.

Der Tod: Gib deine Hand, du schön und zart Gebild!
Bin Freund und komme nicht zu strafen.
Sei gutes Muts! Ich bin nicht wild,
Sollst sanft in meinen Armen schlafen!

Matthias Claudius, 1740–1815

(E. V. Welz, op. 6, no. 2)

Ungeduld, D. 795, no. 7

Ich schnitt' es gern in alle Rinden ein,
Ich grüb es gern in jeden Kieselstein,
Ich möcht es sä'n auf jedes frische Beet
Mit Kressensamen, der es schnell verrät,
Auf jeden weißen Zettel möcht ich's schreiben:
Dein ist mein Herz, und soll es ewig bleiben.

Ich möcht mir ziehen einen jungen Star,
Bis daß er spräch die Worte rein und klar,
Bis er sie spräch mit meines Mundes Klang,
Mit meines Herzens vollem, heißem Drang;
Dann säng er hell durch ihre Fensterscheiben:
Dein ist mein Herz, und soll es ewig bleiben.

Den Morgenwinden möcht ich's hauchen ein,
Ich möcht es säuseln durch den regen Hain;
Oh, leuchtet' es aus jedem Blumenstern!
Trüg es der Duft zu ihr von nah und fern!
Ihr Wogen, könnt ihr nichts als Räder treiben?
Dein ist mein Herz, und soll es ewig bleiben.

I am still young! Go, good man,
and do not touch me!

Death: Give me your hand, lovely and gentle creature!
I am your friend and do not come to punish you.
Be of good cheer! I am not fierce!
You shall sleep softly in my arms!

Impatience

I would carve it on the bark of every tree;
I would chisel it in every stone;
I would sow it in every flower bed,
with watercress, which growing quickly, would give it away;
on every white scrap of paper I would write it:
Thine is my heart, and shall be thine forever!

I would like to teach a young starling
until it would speak the words clearly,
until it would speak with the sound of my voice,
with the full, fervent longing of my heart;
then it would sing clearly through her window:
Thine is my heart, and shall be thine forever;

To the morning wind I would breathe it;
I would whisper it to the quivering trees;
O let it shine from the heart of every flower!
Let its fragrance be born to her from near and far!
O water, can you turn nothing but mill wheels?
Thine is my heart, and shall be thine forever!

Ich meint, es müßt in meinen Augen stehn,
Auf meinen Wangen müßt man's brennen sehn,
Zu lesen wär's auf meinem stummen Mund,
Ein jeder Atemzug gäb's laut ihr kund,
Und sie merkt nichts von all dem bangen Treiben:
Dein ist mein Herz, und soll es ewig bleiben!

Wilhelm Müller, 1794–1827

*(Karl Friedrich Curschmann, op. 3, no. 6; Louis Spohr; Heinrich
Zöllner)*

Der Wanderer, D. 493

Ich komme vom Gebirge her,
Es dampft das Tal, es braust das Meer.
Ich wandle still, bin wenig froh,
Und immer fragt der Seufzer: wo?
Immer wo?
Die Sonne dünkt mich hier so kalt,
Die Blüte welk, das Leben alt,
Und was sie reden, leerer Schall,
Ich bin ein Fremdling überall.

Wo bist du, mein geliebtes Land?
Gesucht, geahnt und nie gekannt!
Das Land, das Land, so hoffnungsgrün,
Das Land, wo meine Rosen blühn,
Wo meine Freunde wandeln gehn,
Wo meine Toten auferstehn,
Das Land, das meine Sprache spricht,
O Land, wo bist du?

Ich wandle still, bin wenig froh,
Und immer fragt der Seufzer: wo?
Immer wo?
Im Geisterhauch tönt's mir zurück:
"Dort, wo du nicht bist, dort ist das Glück!"

Georg Philipp Schmidt (Schmidt von Lübeck), 1766–1849

I should think it must show plainly in my eyes,
on my cheeks anyone must see it burning;
it may be read upon my mute lips;
every breath I draw must proclaim it loudly,
and she notices nothing of all my anxious longing!
Thine is my heart, and shall be thine forever!

The Wanderer

I come here from the mountains;
the valley is damp, the ocean roars.
I wander silent, I am rarely happy,
sighing, I always ask: Where?
Always where?
The sun here seems to me so cold,
the blossoms faded, life old,
and their talk, empty sound;
I am a stranger everywhere.

Where are you, my beloved land?
Sought for, foreseen, and never known!
The land, the land so green with hope,
the land where my roses bloom,
where my friends are walking,
where my dead are resurrected;
the land where they speak my language,
O land, where are you?

I wander silent, I am rarely happy,
sighing, I always ask: Where?
A ghostly breath gives me the answer:
"There where you are not, there is happiness!"

Der Wanderer an den Mond, D. 870

Ich auf der Erd, am Himmel du,
Wir wandern beide rüstig zu:
Ich ernst und trüb, du mild und rein,
Was mag der Unterschied wohl sein?

Ich wandre fremd von Land zu Land,
So heimatlos, so unbekannt;
Berg auf, Berg ab, Wald ein, Wald aus,
Doch bin ich nirgend, ach! zu Haus.

Du aber wanderst auf und ab
Aus Westens Wieg' in Ostens Grab,
Wallst Länder ein und Länder aus,
Und bist doch, wo du bist, zu Haus.

Der Himmel, endlos ausgespannt,
Ist dein geliebtes Heimatland:
O glücklich, wer, wohin er geht,
Doch auf der Heimat Boden steht.

Johann Gabriel Seidl, 1804–75

Wanderers Nachtlied I, D. 224

Der du von dem Himmel bist,
Alles Leid und Schmerzen stillest,
Den, der doppelt elend ist,
Doppelt mit Erquickung füllest,
Ach, ich bin des Treibens müde!
Was soll all der Schmerz und Lust?

The Wanderer to the Moon

I upon earth, you in heaven,
we both go our vigorous ways;
I serious and troubled, you serene and clear—
what can be the difference?

I wander, a stranger, from land to land,
so homeless, so unknown.
Up mountains, down mountains, in and out of the forest,
yet I am never, alas, at home!

But you go your way up and down,
from the cradle in the West to the grave in the East;
you travel from one country to another,
and wherever you are, you are at home!

The boundless heaven
is your beloved homeland;
oh happy is he, who, wherever he goes,
is always at home!

Wanderer's Night Song I

Thou that comest from heaven,
that dost quiet all sorrow and pain,
that dost the doubly wretched
doubly revive,
ah, I am weary of striving!
why all this pain and desire?

Süßer Friede,
Komm, ach komm in meine Brust!

Johann Wolfgang von Goethe, 1749–1832

*(Hugo Wolf; Franz Liszt; Joseph Marx; Johann Georg Reichardt;
Hans Pfitzner, op. 40, no. 5; Nicolai Medtner, op. 15, no. 1;
many others)*

Wanderers Nachtlied II, D. 768

Über allen Gipfeln
Ist Ruh,
In allen Wipfeln
Spürest du

Kaum einen Hauch;
Die Vögelein schweigen im Walde
Warte nur, balde
Ruhest du auch.

Johann Wolfgang von Goethe, 1749–1832

*(Robert Schumann, op. 96, no. 1; Franz Liszt; Carl Friedrich
Zelter; Ferdinand Hiller, op. 129, no. 1; Nicolai Medtner, op. 6,
no. 1; Charles Ives; many others)*

Das Wandern, D. 795, no. 1

Das Wandern ist des Müllers Lust,
Das Wandern!
Das muß ein schlechter Müller sein,
Dem niemals fiel das Wandern ein,
Das Wandern.

Sweet peace,
come, oh come to my breast!

Wanderer's Night Song II

Over all the mountain peaks
is peace,
in all the tree tops
you feel
hardly a breath;
the birds are silent in the forest.
Only wait, soon
you too shall rest.

Roving

Roving is the miller's delight,
Roving!
It is indeed a very poor miller
who has never felt the urge to rove—
roving!

Vom Wasser haben wir's gelernt,
Vom Wasser!
Das hat nicht Rast bei Tag und Nacht,
Ist stets auf Wanderschaft bedacht,
Das Wasser.

Das sehn wir auch den Rädern ab,
Den Rädern!
Die gar nicht gerne stille stehn,
Die sich mein Tag nicht müde drehn,
Die Räder.

Die Steine selbst, so schwer sie sind,
Die Steine!
Sie tanzen mit den muntern Reihn
Und wollen gar noch schneller sein,
Die Steine.

O Wandern, Wandern, meine Lust,
O Wandern!
Herr Meister und Frau Meisterin,
Laßt mich in Frieden weiterziehn
Und wandern.

Wilhelm Müller, 1794–1827

(Heinrich Zöllner)

Das Wirtshaus, D. 911, no. 21

Auf einen Totenacker
Hat mich mein Weg gebracht.
Allhier will ich einkehren,
Hab ich bei mir gedacht.

Ihr grünen Totenkränze
Könnt wohl die Zeichen sein,

From the water we learned this,
from the water!
It does not rest by day or night,
but is always bent on roving,
the water!

We see it too in the millwheels,
the millwheels!
They never want to stop
and never they nor I get tired of turning,
the millwheels!

Even the mill-stones, heavy as they are,
the stones!
They join in the merry dance
and want ever to go faster,
the stones!

O roving, roving, my delight,
o roving!
O master and mistress,
let me go my way in peace,
and rove!

The Inn

Into a graveyard
my way has led me.
Here I will stop,
I thought to myself.

The green memorial wreaths
might well be the signs

Die müde Wandrer laden
Ins kühle Wirtshaus ein.

Sind denn in diesem Hause
Die Kammern all besetzt?
Bin matt zum Niedersinken,
Bin tödlich schwer verletzt.

O unbarmherzge Schenke,
Doch weisest du mich ab?
Nun weiter denn, nur weiter,
Mein treuer Wanderstab!

Wilhelm Müller, 1794–1827

Wohin?, D. 795, no. 2

Ich hört ein Bächlein rauschen
Wohl aus dem Felsenquell,
Hinab zum Tale rauschen
So frisch und wunderhell.

Ich weiß nicht, wie mir wurde,
Nicht, wer den Rat mir gab,
Ich mußte auch hinunter
Mit meinem Wanderstab.

Hinunter und immer weiter,
Und immer dem Bache nach,
Und immer frischer rauschte
Und immer heller der Bach.

Ist das denn meine Straße?
O Bächlein, sprich, wohin?
Du hast mit deinem Rauschen
Mir ganz berauscht den Sinn.

that invite weary travelers
into the cool inn.

Are then in this house
all the rooms taken?
I am so weary I can hardly stand,
and mortally wounded.

O pitiless inn,
do you refuse to take me?
Then on, ever on,
my trusty staff!

Whither?

I heard a brooklet gushing
from a spring among the rocks,
gushing down into the valley,
so fresh and wonderfully clear.

I don't know how it happened,
or who gave me the idea,
but I couldn't resist following it right down
with my walking stick.

Down, always farther,
and always along the bank,
and always brisker
and clearer the brook gushed.

Is this the way I am to go,
tell me, brooklet, whither?
You have, with your gushing,
enchanted my very soul.

Was sag ich denn vom Rauschen?
Das kann kein Rauschen sein:
Es singen wohl die Nixen
Dort unten ihren Reihn.

Laß singen, Gesell, laß rauschen,
Und wandre fröhlich nach!
Es gehn ja Mühlenräder
In jedem klaren Bach.

Wilhelm Müller, 1794–1827

(Ludwig Berger, op. 11, no. 1; Heinrich Zöllner)

What am I saying about gushing?
Gushing it cannot be!
The nixies are singing
and dancing down there.

Sing on, comrade, gush on,
and go your happy way!
There are millwheels turning
in every clear stream.

Robert Schumann

Robert Schumann (1810–56) was a great composer in most fields excepting the opera, and his *lieder* form an important portion of his output. His place as the first successor to Schubert is generally acknowledged. A writer and critic, he was more discriminating than Schubert in his choice of poetry, though he was not always as meticulous as he might have been in his settings. His favorite poets were Heine and Eichendorff.

Die beiden Grenadiere, op. 49, no. 1

Nach Frankreich zogen zwei Grenadier,
Die waren in Rußland gefangen.
Und als sie kamen ins deutsche Quartier,
Sie ließen die Köpfe hangen.

Da hörten sie beide die traurige Mär:
Daß Frankreich verloren gegangen,
Besiegt und geschlagen das tapfere Heer
Und der Kaiser, der Kaiser gefangen!

Da weinten zusammen die Grenadier
Wohl ob der kläglichen Kunde.
Der eine sprach: Wie weh wird mir,
Wie brennt meine alte Wunde!

Der andere sprach: Das Lied ist aus,
Auch ich möcht mit dir sterben,
Doch hab ich Weib und Kind zu Haus,
Die ohne mich verderben.

Was schert mich Weib, was schert mich Kind,
Ich trage weit bessres Verlangen;
Laß sie betteln gehn, wenn sie hungrig sind,—
Mein Kaiser, mein Kaiser gefangen!

Gewähr mir, Bruder, eine Bitt:
Wenn ich jetzt sterben werde,
So nimm meine Leiche nach Frankreich mit,
Begrab mich in Frankreichs Erde.

Das Ehrenkreuz am roten Band
Sollst du aufs Herz mir legen;
Die Flinte gib mir in die Hand,
Und gürt mir um den Degen.

The Two Grenadiers

To France were returning two grenadiers
who had been captured in Russia;
and when they came to the German land
they hung their heads.

For there they heard the sad news
that France was lost,
the great army defeated and destroyed
and the Emperor a prisoner.

The grenadiers wept together
over the miserable tidings.
One spoke: "Woe is me!
How my old wound burns!"

The other said: "It is all over.
I too would like to die with you,
but I have a wife and child at home
who without me would perish.

"What do I care for wife and child?
I have more important concerns.
Let them go begging if they are hungry—
my Emperor is a prisoner!

"Brother, grant me one request
if I must die now;
take my body to France with you,
bury me in French earth.

"My cross of honor, with the red ribbon,
you must lay on my heart;
put my rifle in my hand
and fasten my sword-belt around me.

So will ich liegen und horchen still,
Wie eine Schildwach, im Grabe,
Bis einst ich höre Kanonengebrüll
Und wiehern der Rosse Getrabe.

Dann reitet mein Kaiser wohl über mein Grab,
Viel Schwerter klirren und blitzen;
Dann steig ich gewaffnet hervor aus dem Grab—
Den Kaiser, den Kaiser zu schützen!

Heinrich Heine, 1797–1856

*(Richard Wagner—in Heine's French translation; Karl Gottlieb
Reissiger, op. 95)*

Du bist wie eine Blume, op. 25, no. 24

Du bist wie eine Blume
So hold und schön und rein;
Ich schau dich an, und Wehmut
Schleicht mir ins Herz hinein.

Mir ist, als ob ich die Hände
Aufs Haupt dir legen sollt,
Betend, daß Gott dich erhalte
So rein und schön und hold.

Heinrich Heine, 1797–1856

*(Franz Liszt; Anton Rubinstein, op. 32, no. 5; Sir George
Henschel, op. 37, no. 3; Wilhelm Taubert, op. 186, no. 2;
many others)*

Frühlingsnacht, op. 39, no. 12

Überm Garten durch die Lüfte
Hört ich Wandervögel ziehn,

"So will I lie still and listen,
like a sentry in the grave,
until I hear the noise of cannon
and the hoofs of winnying horses.

"Then should my Emperor ride over my grave,
with many swords clanking and clashing;
then I will arise, fully armed, from my grave,
to defend my Emperor!"

You Are Like a Flower

You are like a flower,
so sweet and fair and chaste;
I look upon you, and melancholy
creeps into my heart.

It seems to me as if I must
lay my hands upon your head,
praying that God will keep you
so chaste, and fair and sweet.

Night in Spring

Over the garden, through the breezes,
I heard passage birds flying:

Das bedeutet Frühlingsdüfte,
Unten fängst's schon an zu blühn.

Jauchzen möcht ich, möchte weinen,
Ist mir's doch, als könnt's nicht sein!
Alte Wunder wieder scheinen
Mit dem Mondesglanz herein.

Und der Mond, die Sterne sagen's,
Und im Traume rauscht's der Hain,
Und die Nachtigallen schlagen's:
Sie ist deine, sie ist dein!

Joseph, Freiherr von Eichendorff, 1788–1857

(Adolf Jensen, op. 1, no. 6; Heinrich Marschner, op. 144, no. 1;
Karl Friedrich Curschmann, op. 25, no. 1; others)

Ich grolle nicht, op. 48, no. 7

Ich grolle nicht, und wenn das Herz auch bricht,
Ewig verlornes Lieb! ich grolle nicht.
Wie du auch strahlst in Diamantenpracht,
Es fällt kein Strahl in deines Herzens Nacht.

Das weiß ich längst. Ich sah dich ja im Traume,
Und sah die Nacht in deines Herzens Raume,
Und sah die Schlang, die dir am Herzen frißt,
Ich sah, mein Lieb, wie sehr du elend bist.

Heinrich Heine, 1797–1856

(Charles Ives, others)

that presages fragrant spring.
Underfoot the flowers are already beginning to bloom.

I want to shout for joy! I want to weep!
I cannot believe what I feel!
Old wonders appear again
in the light of the moon.

And the moon, the stars, are telling it,
and in dreams the grove rustles it;
and the nightingales peal it forth—
She is yours! She is yours!

I Bear No Grudge

I bear no grudge, even though my heart may break,
eternally lost love! I bear no grudge.
However you may shine in the splendor of your diamonds
no ray of light falls in the darkness of your heart.

I have long known this. I saw you in a dream,
and saw the night within the void of your heart,
and saw the serpent that is eating your heart—
I saw, my love, how very miserable you are.

Im Rhein, im heiligen Strome, op. 48, no. 6

Im Rhein, im heiligen Strome,
Da spiegelt sich in den Welln,
Mit seinem großen Dome,
Das große, heilige Köln.

Im Dom, da steht ein Bildnis,
Auf goldenem Leder gemalt;
In meines Lebens Wildnis
Hat's freundlich hineingestrahlt.

Es schweben Blumen und Englein
Um Unsre Liebe Frau;
Die Augen, die Lippen, die Wänglein,
Die gleichen der Liebsten genau.

Heinrich Heine, 1797–1856

(Robert Franz, op. 18, no. 2; Franz Liszt, 1856; A. M. Foerster;
Heinrich Proch; others)

Im wunderschönen Monat Mai, op. 48, no. 1

Im wunderschönen Monat Mai,
Als alle Knospen sprangen,
Da ist in meinem Herzen
Die Liebe aufgegangen.

Im wunderschönen Monat Mai,
Als alle Vögel sangen,
Da hab ich ihr gestanden
Mein Sehnen und Verlangen.

Heinrich Heine, 1797–1856

(Robert Franz, op. 25, no. 5; Victor Nessler, op. 21, no. 1; David
Popper, op. 2, no. 1; Henry K. Hadley; Ethelbert Nevin, op. 2,
no. 2; many others)

The Rhine, the Holy River

The Rhine, the holy river,
reflects in its waves,
with its great cathedral,
the great holy city of Cologne.

In the cathedral there hangs a painting,
painted on gilded leather;
in the confusion of my life
it has shone kindly down on me.

Flowers and cherubs float
about Our dear Lady.
Her eyes, her lips, her cheeks
are exactly like those of my love.

In the Lovely Month of May

In the lovely month of May,
when all the buds were bursting,
then within my heart
love burst forth.

In the lovely month of May,
when all the birds were singing,
then I confessed to her
my longing and my desire.

Die Lotosblume, op. 25, no. 7

Die Lotosblume ängstigt
Sich vor der Sonne Pracht,
Und mit gesenktem Haupte
Erwartet sie träumend die Nacht.

Der Mond, der ist ihr Buhle,
Er weckt sie mit seinem Licht,
Und ihm entschleiert sie freundlich
Ihr frommes Blumengesicht.

Sie blüht und glüht und leuchtet
Und starret stumm in die Höh;
Sie duftet und weinet und zittert
Vor Liebe und Liebesweh.

Heinrich Heine, 1797–1856

(Robert Franz, op. 25, no. 1; Carl Loewe, op. 9; Wilhelm Kienzl,
op. 8, no. 1; Charles Ives; others)

Mondnacht, op. 39, no. 5

Es war, als hätt der Himmel
Die Erde still geküßt,
Daß sie im Blütenschimmer
Von ihm nur träumen müßt.

Die Luft ging durch die Felder,
Die Ähren wogten sacht,
Es rauschten leis die Wälder,
So sternklar war die Nacht.

Und meine Seele spannte
Weit ihre Flügel aus,

The Lotus Flower

The lotus flower is fretful
before the glory of the sun,
and with her head hanging
waits, dreaming, for the night.

The moon, who is her lover,
wakes her with his light,
and for him she smilingly unveils
her innocent flower-face.

She blooms and glows and gleams,
and gazes silently upward;
she exhales her fragrance, and weeps, and trembles,
with love and love's torment.

Moonlit Night

It seemed as though the heavens
had kissed the earth to silence,
so that, amid glistening flowers,
she must now dream heavenly dreams.

The breeze passed through the fields;
the corn stirred softly;
the forest rustled lightly,
so clear and starry was the night.

And my soul spread
wide its wings;

Flog durch die stillen Lande,
Als flöge sie nach Haus.

Joseph, Freiherr von Eichendorff, 1788–1857

(Johannes Brahms; Heinrich Marschner, op. 179, no. 2; Emanuel
Moór, op. 43, no. 1; Eduard Lassen; others)

Der Nussbaum, op. 25, no. 3

Es grünet ein Nussbaum vor dem Haus,
Duftig,
Luftig
Breitet er blättrig die Äste aus.

Viel liebliche Blüten stehen d'ran;
Linde
Winde
Kommen, sie herzlich zu umfahn.

Es flüstern je zwei zu zwei gepaart,
Neigend,
Beugend
Zierlich zum Kusse die Häuptchen zart.

Sie flüstern von einem Mägdlein, das
Dächte
Nächte
Tagelang, wüsste, ach! selber nicht was.

Sie flüstern,—wer mag verstehn so gar
Leise
Weise?
Flüstern von Bräut'gam und nächstem Jahr.

took flight through the silent land
as though it were flying home.

The Nut Tree

A nut tree grows in front of the house;
fragrant,
airy·
it stretches out its leafy boughs.

Many lovely blossoms grow on it;
gentle
winds
come to fan them affectionately.

They whisper continuously two by two,
bowing,
bending
prettily their soft little heads for a kiss.

They whisper about a girl who sits
meditating
night
and day, she herself doesn't know what about.

They whisper—who could understand
so soft
a tune?—
whisper of a bridegroom in the year to come.

Das Mägdlein horchet, es rauscht im Baum;
Sehnend,
Wähnend,
Sinkt es lächelnd in Schlaf und Traum.

Julius Mosen, 1803–67

Der Soldat, op. 40, no. 3

Es geht bei gedämpfter Trommel Klang;
Wie weit noch die Stätte! der Weg wie lang!
O wär' er zur Ruh und alles vorbei!
Ich glaub', es bricht mir das Herz entzwei.

Ich hab' in der Welt nur ihn geliebt,
Nur ihn, dem jetzt man den Tod doch giebt.
Bei klingendem Spiele wird paradiert,
Dazu bin auch ich kommandiert.

Nun schaut er auf zum letzenmal
In Gottes Sonne freudigen Strahl,
Nun binden sie ihm die Augen zu—
Dir schenke Gott die ewige Ruh!

Es haben die Neun wohl angelegt,
Acht Kugeln haben vorbeigefegt;
Sie zitterten alle vor Jammer und Schmerz—
Ich aber, ich traf ihn mitten ins Herz.

Adalbert von Chamisso, 1781–1838 (after Hans Christian
Andersen)

(Friedrich Silcher; Edvard Grieg)

The girl listens to the rustling in the tree;
longing,
imagining,
she sinks smiling into sleep and dreams.

The Soldier

It is done to the sound of muffled drums;
how distant, still, the place! How long the way!
Oh if only he were at rest and all were over!
I believe it will break my heart in two.

In all the world I loved him only,
him only whom they now put to death.
With music and ceremony there will be a parade,
and I too am ordered to take part.

Now he looks up for the last time
in the joyous light of God's sun;
Now they are blindfolding him—
God send you eternal rest!

The nine have taken good aim;
eight bullets have missed him.
They were all trembling with distress and pain—
but I, I shot straight to his heart.

Stille Tränen, op. 35, no. 10

Du bist vom Schlaf erstanden
Und wandelst durch die Au.
Da liegt ob allen Landen
Der Himmel wunderblau.

So lang du ohne Sorgen
Geschlummert schmerzenlos,
Der Himmel bis zum Morgen
Viel Tränen niedergoß.

In stillen Nächten weinet
Oft mancher aus den Schmerz,
Und morgens dann ihr meinet,
Stets fröhlich sei sein Herz.

Justinius Andreas Christian Kerner, 1786–1862

(Fritz Helmsdorf; Alexander Winterberger, op. 91, no. 17)

Waldesgespräch, op. 39, no. 3

Es ist schon spät, es ist schon kalt,
Was reitest du einsam durch den Wald?
Der Wald ist lang, du bist allein,
Du schöne Braut! Ich führ dich heim!—

"Groß ist der Männer Trug und List,
Vor Schmerz mein Herz gebrochen ist,
Wohl irrt das Waldhorn her und hin,
O flieh! Du weißt nicht, wer ich bin."—

So reich geschmückt ist Roß und Weib,
So wunderschön der junge Leib,
Jetzt kenn ich dich—Gott steh mir bei!
Du bist die Hexe Lorelei—

Silent Tears

You have arisen from sleep
and walk through the meadow.
Over all the land lies
the wonderful blue of heaven.

While without care
you slept free of pain,
before morning heaven has
poured down many tears.

In quiet nights many
often weep for grief,
and in the morning you believe
their hearts are always happy.

Dialogue in the Forest

"It is already late, it is growing cold;
why do you ride alone through the wood?
The forest is vast, you are alone.
Beautiful bride! I will see you home!"

"Great are the deceit and the cunning of men;
my heart is wracked with pain.
The sound of the horn is all around us.
Begone! You do not know who I am."

"So richly adorned are both horse and lady,
so enchanting is your young body—
now I know you—God be with me!—
You are the sorceress Lorelei."

"Du kennst mich wohl—vom hohen Stein
Schaut still mein Schloß tief in den Rhein.
Es ist schon spät, es ist schon kalt,
Kommst nimmermehr aus diesem Wald!"

Joseph, Freiherr von Eichendorff, 1788–1857

(Adolf Jensen, op. 5, no. 4; Hans Sommer; Alexander von Zemlinsky, 1895; others)

Wanderlied, op. 35, no. 3

Wohlauf! noch getrunken den funkelnden Wein!
Ade nun, ihr Lieben! geschieden muß sein.
Ade nun, ihr Berge, du väterlich Haus!
Es treibt in die Ferne mich mächtig hinaus.

Die Sonne, sie bleibet am Himmel nicht stehn,
Es treibt sie durch Länder und Meere zu gehn.
Die Woge nicht haftet am einsamen Strand,
Die Stürme, sie brausen mit Macht durch das Land.

Mit eilenden Wolken der Vogel dort zieht
Und singt in der Ferne ein heimatlich Lied,
So treibt es den Burschen durch Wälder und Feld,
Zu gleichen der Mutter, der wandernden Welt.

Da grüßen ihn Vögel bekannt überm Meer,
Sie flogen von Fluren der Heimat hieher;
Da duften die Blumen vertraulich um ihn,
Sie trieben vom Lande die Lüfte dahin.

Die Vögel, die kennen sein väterlich Haus,
Die Blumen, die pflanzt er der Liebe zum Strauß,
Und Liebe, die folgt ihm, sie geht ihm zur Hand:
So wird ihm zur Heimat das ferneste Land.

Justinius Andreas Christian Kerner, 1786–1862

(Ludwig Erk)

"You Know me well—from a high cliff
my castle looks silently deep into the Rhine.
It is already late, it is growing cold.
Nevermore shall you leave this wood!"

Wander-Song

Come, let us drain
the sparkling wine!
Farewell, companions,
now we must part!
Farewell to the mountains,
and to my father's house!
I feel an irresistible urge
to roam.

The sun does not stand
still in the heavens,
but feels the impulse
to wander, over land and sea.
The wave is not fixed
to the lonely shore;
the storm blusters mightily
throughout the land.

With the hurrying clouds
up there the bird moves
and sings in the distance
a song of home.
So youth is impelled
through forest and field,
as is our mother,
the moving world.

There birds greet him
that he has known over seas;
they have flown here
from the meadows of home.
There the fragrance of the flowers
around him is familiar;
the breezes blow it
from his country.

The birds know
his father's house;
the flowers he once planted
to make a posy for his love,
and the love that follows him
and is near at hand;
so the most distant country
becomes a home to him.

Widmung, 2 op. 25, no. 1

Du meine Seele, du mein Herz,
Du meine Wonn, o du mein Schmerz,
Du meine Welt, in der ich lebe,
Mein Himmel du, darein ich schwebe,
O du mein Grab, in das hinab
Ich ewig meinen Kummer gab.
Du bist die Ruh, du bist der Frieden,
Du bist vom Himmel mir beschieden.
Daß du mich liebst, macht mich mir wert,
Dein Blick hat mich vor mir verklärt,
Du hebst mich liebend über mich,
Mein guter Geist, mein beßres Ich!

Friedrich Rückert, 1788–1866

*(Heinrich Marschner, op. 106, no. 4; Henry Charles Litolff,
op. 58, no. 1)*

Dedication

You my soul, you my heart,
you my joy, you my grief;
you my world in which I live,
my heaven you, into which I soar;
o you my grave in which
I bury forever my sorrows.
You are rest, you are consolation,
you are given to me from heaven.
That you love me makes me worthy in my own eyes;
your glance transfigures me in my own sight;
you raise me lovingly above myself—
my guardian spirit, my better self.

Richard Strauss

Richard Strauss (1864–1949), married to a singer, was a prolific composer of songs. Considered a radical in his young days and more recently a reactionary, he has never wanted for critics, whether as an opera composer or as a purveyor of orchestral tone poems. Some have blasted him for his taste in poetry, but perhaps this is unjust. Strauss avoided poems that he felt had already been adequately set, and thus there was little left for him in Goethe, Heine, Eichendorff, and the other regulars. Bierbaum, Mackay, Dahn, and Henckell were his contemporaries, and he found in them the inspiration he needed. Whatever the verdict may have been during his lifetime, there is no question that the Strauss songs have stood the test of time, and there is still an enthusiastic public for them.

Allerseelen, op. 10, no. 8

Stell auf den Tisch die duftenden Reseden,
Die letzten roten Astern trag herbei,
Und laß uns wieder von der Liebe reden,
Wie einst im Mai.

Gib mir die Hand, daß ich sie heimlich drücke
Und wenn man's sieht, mir ist es einerlei,
Gib mir nur einen deiner süßen Blicke,
Wie einst im Mai.

Es blüht und duftet heut auf jedem Grabe,
Ein Tag im Jahr ist ja den Toten frei,
Komm an mein Herz, daß ich dich wieder habe,
Wie einst im Mai.

Hermann von Gilm zu Rosenegg, 1812–64

(Eduard Lassen, op. 85, no. 3; Ludwig Thuille, op. 44, no. 4;
Joseph Pembauer, op. 33, no. 2; many others)

Befreit, op. 39, no. 4

Du wirst nicht weinen. Leise, leise
Wirst du lächeln; und wie zur Reise
Geb' ich dir Blick und Kuss zurück.
Unsre lieben vier Wände! Du hast sie bereitet,
Ich habe sie dir zur Welt geweitet—
O Glück!

Dann wirst du heiss meine Hände fassen
Und wirst mir deine Seele lassen,
Lässt unsern Kindern mich zurück.
Du schenkest mir dein ganzes Leben,
Ich will es ihnen wiedergeben—
O Glück!

All Souls' Day

Place on the table the fragrant mignonettes,
bring in the last red asters,
and let us speak again of love,
as once in May.

Give me your hand, that I may secretly press it,
and if anyone sees, that matters not to me.
Give me only one of your sweet glances,
as once in May.

Every grave blooms and breathes fragrance tonight:
one day in the year belongs to the dead.
Come to my heart, that I may hold you again,
as once in May.

Released

You will not cry, gently, gently
you will smile, and as though going on a journey
I will return your glance and your kiss.
Our beloved four walls! You made them ready;
I have made them a world for you—
O happiness!

Then you must warmly clasp my hands
and leave your soul with me,
as you leave me to our children.
You gave me your whole life;
I shall give it back to them—
O happiness!

Es wird sehr bald sein, wir wissen's beide.
Wir haben einander befreit vom Leide;
So geb' ich dich der Welt zurück.
Dann wirst du mir nur noch im Traum erscheinen
Und mich segnen und mit mir weinen—
O Glück!

Richard Dehmel, 1863–1920

Breit über mein Haupt, op. 19, no. 2

Breit über mein Haupt dein schwarzes Haar,
Neig zu mir dein Angesicht,
Da strömt in die Seele so hell und klar
Mir deine Augen Licht.

Ich will nicht droben der Sonne Pracht
Noch der Sterne leuchtenden Kranz,
Ich will nur deiner Locken Nacht
Und deine Blicke Glanz.

Adolf Friedrich, Graf von Schack, 1815–94

Freundliche Vision, op. 48, no. 1

Nicht im Schlafe hab ich das geträumt,
Hell am Tage sah ichs schön vor mir:
Eine Wiese voller Margeritten;
Tief ein weisses Haus in grünen Büschen;
Götterbilder leuchten aus dem Laube.
Und ich geh mit Einer, die mich lieb hat,
Ruhigen Gemütes in die Kühle
Dieses weissen Hauses, in den Frieden,
Der voll Schönheit wartet, dass wir kommen.

Otto Julius Bierbaum, 1865–1910

(Max Reger, op. 66, no. 2)

It will be very soon, we both know it.
We have set each other free from sorrow;
so I give you back to the world.
Then you will come to me again only in dreams,
and bless me and weep with me—
O happiness!

Spread Over My Head

Spread over my head your black hair,
incline to me your face,
it streams in my soul so bright and clear,
the light of your eyes.
I don't seek there the glory of the sun,
nor the shining crown of the stars;
I want only the night of your tresses
and the radiance of your glance.

Pleasant Reverie

Not in sleep did I dream this;
in broad daylight I saw it beautiful before me:
a meadow full of daisies,
a white house deep in the green bushes;
sculptured gods shine through the foliage.
And I walk with one who loves me,
my soul content in the cool
of this white house, where peace,
full of beauty, awaits our coming.

Heimkehr, op. 15, no. 5

Leiser schwanken die Äste,
Der Kahn fliegt uferwärts,
Heim kehrt die Taube zum Neste,
Zu dir kehrt heim mein Herz.

Genug am schimmernden Tage,
Wenn rings das Leben lärmt,
Mit irrem Flügelschlage
Ist es ins Weite geschwärmt.

Doch nun die Sonne geschieden,
Und stille sich senkt auf den Hain,
Fühlt es: bei dir ist der Frieden,
Die Ruh' bei dir allein.

Adolf Friedrich, Graf von Schack, 1815–94

Heimliche Aufforderung, op. 27, no. 3

Auf, hebe die funkelnde Schale empor zum Mund,
Und trinke beim Freudenmahle dein Herze gesund.
Und wenn du sie hebst, so winke mir heimlich zu,
Dann lächle ich und dann trinke ich still wie du. . . .

Und still gleich mir betrachte um uns das Heer
Der trunknen Schwätzer—verachte sie nicht zu sehr.
Nein, hebe die blinkende Schale, gefüllt mit Wein,
Und laß beim lärmenden Mahle sie glücklich sein.

Doch hast du das Mahl genossen, den Durst gestillt,
Dann verlasse der lauten Genossen festfreudiges Bild,
Und wandle hinaus in den Garten zum Rosenstrauch,
Dort will ich dich dann erwarten nach altem Brauch,

Homecoming

Lightly rustle the branches,
the boat hurries to the shore,
home returns the dove to its nest,
to you my heart returns home.

Enough in the gleaming day
if all around us life is noisy,
[my heart] on wings
flies into the distance.

But now the sun has gone down,
and silently sinks in the grove.
It feels: with you is peace,
rest with you alone.

Secret Invitation

Up, raise the sparkling bowl
to your lips,
and drink at the feast,
that your heart may be healed.

no, raise the glittering bowl,
filled with wine,
and let them at their noisy meal
be happy.

And as you lift it up, give me
a secret sign,
then I shall smile and drink
silently as you.

But when you have had your fill
and quenched your thirst,
then leave your loud companions
to the festive scene.

And, silent as I, consider
around us the crowd
of drunken babblers—do not despise
them too much;

Und will an die Brust dir sinken, eh du's gehofft,
Und deine Küsse trinken, wie ehmals oft,
Und flechten in deine Haare der Rosen Pracht.
O komm, du wunderbare, ersehnte Nacht!

John Henry Mackay, 1864–1933

(Eugen d'Albert, op. 21, no. 1)

Morgen, op. 27, no. 4

Und morgen wird die Sonne wieder scheinen
Und auf dem Wege, den ich gehen werde,
Wird uns, die Glücklichen, sie wieder einen
Inmitten dieser sonnenatmenden Erde. . . .

Und zu dem Strand, dem weiten, wogenblauen,
Werden wir still und langsam niedersteigen,
Stumm werden wir uns in die Augen schauen,
Und auf uns sinkt des Glückes stummes Schweigen. . . .

John Henry Mackay, 1864–1933

Die Nacht, op. 10, no. 3

Aus dem Walde tritt die Nacht,
Aus den Bäumen schleicht sie leise,
Schaut sich um in weitem Kreise,
Nun gib acht.

Alle Lichter dieser Welt,
Alle Blumen, alle Farben löscht sie aus
Und stiehlt die Garben weg
Vom Feld.

And go out into the garden,
to the rosebush;
there I will be waiting for you,
as I used to do,

and will sink upon your breast
before you expect it,
and drink your kisses
as I often used to do,

and will twine in your hair
the splendor of the rose—
o come, wondrous,
longed-for night!

Tomorrow

And tomorrow the sun will shine again,
and on the path that I shall follow
it will reunite us, the blessed ones,
amidst the sun-breathing world.

And to the shore, broad and blue with the waves,
we shall go down quietly and slowly.
Mute, we shall look into each other's eyes,
and upon us will descend the great silence of happiness.

The Night

Out of the forest steals the night,
out of the trees she slinks quietly,
looks round about—
now take care!

All the lights of this world,
all flowers, all colors
she extinguishes, and steals the sheaves
away from the fields.

Alles nimmt sie, was nur hold,
Nimmt das Silber weg des Stroms,
Nimmt vom Kupferdach des Doms
Weg das Gold.

Ausgeplündert steht der Strauch,
Rücke näher, Seel an Seele;
O die Nacht, mir bangt, sie stehle
Dich mir auch.

Hermann von Gilm zu Rosenegg, 1812–64

Ruhe, Meine Seele, op. 27, no. 1

Nicht ein Lüftchen
Regt sich leise,
Sanft entschlummert
Ruht der Hain;
Durch der Blätter
Dunkle Hülle
Stiehlt sich lichter
Sonnenschein.

Ruhe, ruhe,
Meine Seele,
Deine Stürme
Gingen wild,
Hast getobt und
Hast gezittert,
Wie die Brandung,
Wenn sie schwillt!
Diese Zeiten
Sind gewaltig,
Bringen Herz und
Hirn in Not—
Ruhe, ruhe,

She takes away all that is pleasing—
the silver from the river;
from the copper roof of the cathedral
she steals the gold.

The shrubbery stands pundered—
come closer, soul to soul!
o the night, I fear, will steal
you too from me!

Rest, My Soul

Not a breeze
is lightly stirring;
in soft sleep
the grove is at rest;
through the leaves'
dark cover
steal bright shafts of
sunshine.
Rest, rest,
my soul,
your storms
have raged wildly;
you have started up
and have trembled
like the seething
breakers!
These times
are portentous,
they try the heart
and the brain to extremity—
rest, rest,

Meine Seele,
Und vergiss,
Was dich bedroht!

Karl Henckell, 1864–1929

Schlechtes Wetter, op. 69, no. 5

Das ist ein schlechtes Wetter,
Es regnet und stürmt und schneit;
Ich sitze am Fenster und schaue
Hinaus in die Dunkelheit.

Da schimmert ein einsames Lichtchen,
Das wandelt langsam fort;
Ein Mütterchen mit dem Laternchen
Wankt über die Straße dort.

Ich glaube, Mehl und Eier
Und Butter kaufte sie ein;
Sie will einen Kuchen backen
Fürs große Töchterlein.

Die liegt zu Haus im Lehnstuhl,
Und blinzelt schläfrig ins Licht;
Die goldnen Locken wallen
Über das süße Gesicht.

Heinrich Heine, 1797–1856

Ständchen, op. 17, no. 2

Mach auf, mach auf, doch leise, mein Kind,
Um keinen vom Schlummer zu wecken.

my soul,
and forget
the things that threaten you!

Terrible Weather

The weather is terrible—
it is raining, storming and snowing.
I sit in the window and gaze
out into the darkness.

One lone light glimmers
and moves slowly on;
a little mother with a little lantern
staggers across the street there.

I believe she's bought flour and eggs
and butter;
she is going to bake a cake
for her big little daughter.

who lies at home in an easy chair
and blinks sleepily in the light,
her golden hair falling
over her sweet face.

Serenade

Open! Open! But softly, my child,
that you wake no one from sleep!

Kaum murmelt der Bach, kaum zittert im Wind
Ein Blatt an den Büschen und Hecken.
Drum leise, mein Mädchen, daß nichts sich regt,
Nur leise die Hand auf die Klinke gelegt.

Mit Tritten, wie Tritte der Elfen so sacht,
Um über die Blumen zu hüpfen,
Flieg leicht hinaus in die Mondscheinnacht,
Zu mir in den Garten zu schlüpfen.
Rings schlummern die Blüten am rieselnden Bach
Und duften im Schlaf, nur die Liebe ist wach.

Sitz nieder, hier dämmert's geheimnisvoll
Unter den Lindenbäumen,
Die Nachtigall uns zu Häupten soll
Von unseren Küssen träumen
Und die Rose, wenn sie am Morgen erwacht,
Hoch glühn von den Wonneschauern der Nacht.

Adolf Friedrich, Graf von Schack, 1815–94

*(Hugo Berger, op. 5, no. 2; Robert Kahn, op. 12, no. 2; Julius
Schaeffer, op. 18, no. 6; others)*

Traum durch die Dämmerung, op. 29, no. 1

Weite Wiesen im Dämmergrau;
Die Sonne verglomm, die Sterne ziehn,
Nun geh ich hin zu der schönsten Frau,
Weit über Wiesen im Dämmergrau,
Tief in den Busch von Jasmin.

Durch Dämmergrau in der Liebe Land;
Ich gehe nicht schnell, ich eile nicht;
Mich zieht ein weiches, samtenes Band
Durch Dämmergrau in der Liebe Land,
In ein blaues, mildes Licht.

Otto Julius Bierbaum, 1865–1910

(Max Reger, op. 35, no. 3; Christian Sinding)

The brook hardly murmurs, the wind hardly stirs
a leaf on the bushes and lattices.
Then softly, my dear, that nothing may move,
lay your hand lightly on the latch.

With footsteps as light as the steps of elves
skipping over the flowers,
fly lightly into the moonlight night
as you slip out to me in the garden!
Around us the flowers slumber by the rippling brook
and exhale their fragrance in their sleep; only love is awake.

Sit down! Here dusk is falling mysteriously
under the linden trees.
The nightingale above our heads shall
dream of our kisses;
and the rose, when she awakes tomorrow,
shall bloom more sublimely after the rapture of the night.

Dreaming through the Twilight

Broad meadows in the twilight gray;
the sun has set, the stars appear.
Now I go to the loveliest of women,
far over the meadows in the twilight gray,
deep into the jasmine bush

Through the twilight gray to the land of love,
I do not go quickly, I do not hurry,
drawn by a fragile velvet ribbon,
through the twilight gray to the land of love,
into a blue, soft light.

Waldseligkeit, op. 49, no. 1

Der Wald beginnt zu rauschen,
Den Bäumen naht die Nacht;
Als ob sie selig lauschen,
Berühren sie sich sacht.

Und unter ihren Zweigen
Da bin ich ganz allein.
Da bin ich ganz mein eigen:
Ganz nur dein.

Richard Dehmel, 1863–1920

(Joseph Marx, 1911; Max Reger, op. 62, no. 2; Alma Mahler)

Wiegenlied, op. 41, no. 1

Träume, träume du mein süßes Leben,
Von dem Himmel, der die Blumen bringt.
Blüten schimmern da, die leben
Von dem Lied, das deine Mutter singt.

Träume, träume, Knospe meiner Sorgen,
Von dem Tage, da die Blume sproß;
Von dem hellen Blütenmorgen,
Da dein Seelchen sich der Welt erschloß.

Träume, träume, Blüte meiner Liebe,
Von der stillen, von der heilgen Nacht,
Da die Blume seiner Liebe
Diese Welt zum Himmel mir gemacht.

Richard Dehmel, 1863–1920

(Hans Pfitzner, op. 11, no. 4)

Happiness in the Forest

The woods begin to rustle,
the night comes to the trees;
as if blissfully listening
they are gently coming to rest.

And under their branches
I am quite alone—
there I am all to myself,
only yours, yours alone.

Cradle Song

Dream, dream, my sweet life,
of heaven, which brings the flowers;
blossoms glisten there, they quiver
to the song your mother sings.

Dream, dream, bud of my care,
of the day when the flowers sprouted,
of the bright blossoming morning
when your little soul came into the world.

Dream, dream, bloom of my love,
of the silent holy night
when the flowering of his love
made this world a heaven for me.

Zueignung, op. 10, no. 1

Ja, du weißt es, teure Seele,
Daß ich fern von dir mich quäle,
Liebe macht die Herzen krank,
Habe Dank.

Einst hielt ich, der Freiheit Zecher,
Hoch den Amethystenbecher
Und du segnetest den Trank,
Habe Dank.

Und beschworst darin die Bösen,
Bis ich, was ich nie gewesen,
Heilig, heilig ans Herz dir sank,
Habe Dank.

Hermann von Gilm zu Rosenegg, 1812–64

Devotion

Yes, you know it, dear soul,
that when I am away from you I am miserable;
love makes the heart sick.
Take my thanks.

Did not I, the tippler of liberty,
hold high the amethist cup,
and you bless the draught?
Take my thanks.

And you exorcised the evil within it,
until I, blessed as I had never been,
sank upon your heart.
Take my thanks.

Richard Wagner

The few songs of Richard Wagner (1813–83) are not among his most important compositions, but they have a place in the *lieder* repertoire. His very early settings of poems from Goethe's *Faust* are of historical interest. His most significant contribution was a set of *Fünf Gedichte* to poems of Mathilde Wesendonck—two of them designated studies for *Tristan und Isolde,* the rest containing echoes of his other mature works.

Schmerzen

Sonne, weinest jeden Abend
Dir die schönen Augen rot,
Wenn im Meeresspiegel badend
Dich erreicht der frühe Tod;

Doch erstehst in alter Pracht,
Glorie der düsteren Welt,
Du am Morgen neu erwacht,
Wie ein stolzer Siegesheld!

Ach, wie sollte ich da klagen,
Wie, mein Herz, so schwer dich sehn,
Muss die Sonne selbst verzagen,
Muss die Sonne untergehn?

Und gebieret Tod nur Leben,
Geben Schmerzen Wonne nur:
O wie dank ich, das gegeben
Solche Schmerzen mir, Natur!

Mathilde Wesendonck, 1828–1902

Träume
(Studie zu Tristan und Isolde)

Sag, welch wunderbare Träume
Halten meinen Sinn umfangen,
Daß sie nicht wie leere Schäume
Sind in ödes Nichts vergangen?

Träume, die in jeder Stunde,
Jedem Tage schöner blühn,
Und mit ihrer Himmelskunde
Selig durchs Gemüte ziehn!

Torments

Sun, you weep every evening
until your beautiful eyes are red,
when bathing in the mirror of the sea
early death overtakes you.

Yet you arise in your old splendor,
the glory of the sullen world;
you, in the morning newly awakened
like a proud battle hero.

Ah, how I should lament,
my heart, as you seem so heavy.
Must the sun itself despair—
must the sun set?

And if death begets only life
and torment gives only bliss,
O how thankful I am that
nature has given me such torments!

Dreams
(Study for Tristan and Isolde)

Say, what wonderful dreams
hold my senses captive,
so that they do not, like empty foam,
vanish into nothingness?

Dreams, that in every hour,
every day, become more beautiful,
and with their heavenly message
blessedly pass through my mind!

Träume, die wie hehre Strahlen
In die Seele sich versenken,
Dort ein ewig Bild zu malen:
Allvergessen, Eingedenken!

Träume, wie wenn Frühlingssonne
Aus dem Schnee die Blüten küßt,
Daß zu nie geahnter Wonne
Sie der neue Tag Begrüßt,

Daß sie wachsen, daß sie blühen,
Träumend spenden ihren Duft,
Sanft an deiner Brust verglühen,
Und dann sinken in die Gruft.

Mathilde Wesendonck, 1828–1902

Dreams, which like sublime rays
submerge in my soul,
there to paint an eternal picture,
forgetting all, mindful of one!

Dreams, as when the sun of spring
kisses the flowers from out the snow,
so that to unforeseen bliss
the new day greets them,

so that they grow, that they bloom,
dreaming, lavish their fragrance,
gently perish on your breast
and then sink into the grave.

Hugo Wolf

Though his work is almost exclusively in the field of *lieder*—except for one opera and a few choral and instrumental works—Hugo Wolf (1860–1903) takes his place among the supreme masters of music because of the perfection of his limited output. He worked spasmodically at white heat, concentrating on a single poet until he had exhausted the lyrics that inspired him, setting words in what seemed the natural music of speech, and underlining this with vividly descriptive piano parts.

Abschied

Unangeklopft ein Herr tritt abends bei mir ein:
"Ich hab die Ehr, Ihr Rezensent zu sein."
Sofort nimmt er das Licht in die Hand,
Besieht lang meinen Schatten an der Wand,
Rückt nah und fern: "Nun, lieber junger Mann,
Sehn Sie doch gefälligst mal Ihre Nas so von der Seite an!
Sie geben zu, daß das ein Auswuchs is."
—Das? Alle Wetter—gewiß!
Ei Hasen! ich dachte nicht,
All mein Legtage nicht,
Daß ich so eine Weltnase führt' im Gesicht!

Der Mann sprach noch verschiednes hin und her,
Ich weiß, auf meine Ehre, nicht mehr;
Meinte vielleicht, ich sollt ihm beichten.
Zuletzt stand er auf; ich tat ihm leuchten.
Wie wir nun an der Treppe sind,
Da geb ich ihm, ganz froh gesinnt,
Einen kleinen Tritt
Nur so von hinten aufs Gesäße mit—
Alle Hagel! ward das ein Gerumpel,
Ein Gepurzel, ein Gehumpel!
Dergleichen hab ich nie gesehn,
All mein Lebtage nicht gesehn,
Einen Menschen so rasch die Treppn hinabgehn!

Eduard Friedrich Mörike, 1804–75

Anakreons Grab

Wo die Rose hier blüht, wo Reben um Lorbeer sich schlingen,
Wo das Turtelchen lockt, wo sich das Grillchen ergötzt,
Welch ein Grab ist hier, das alle Götter mit Leben

Parting

Without knocking a man one evening entered my lodgings.
"I have the honor to be your critic."
Immediately he took the lamp in his hand;
inspecting at length my shadow on the wall,
he moved back and forth: "Now, my dear young man,
do me the favor to look at your nose from this side!
You will grant that it is not normal."
"That? Good gracious—really!"
My word! I never realized
that I carried a world-wonder on my face!

The man spoke about this and that—
on my honor, I don't know what else;
perhaps he thought I should make a confession to him.
Finally he got up; I lighted him out.
As we stood at the head of the stairs
I gave him mischievously
a little kick,
just so, from behind on his seat—
Goodness! What a rattling!
What a tumbling! What a limping!
I never saw the like,
in all my life I never saw
a man go downstairs so quickly!

Anacreon's Grave

Here where the roses bloom, where vine and laurel intertwine,
where the turtle-dove coos, where the grasshopper rejoices,
what grave is this that all the gods have planted beautifully

Schön bepflanzt und geziert? Es ist Anakreons Ruh.
Frühling, Sommer und Herbst genoß der glückliche Dichter;
Vor dem Winter hat ihn endlich der Hügel geschützt.

Johann Wolfgang von Goethe, 1749–1832

(Alfred Velentin Reuss; Fartein Valen, op. 3, no. 2; Nikolaus
Janowski; P. Meyendorff)

Auch kleine Dinge

Auch kleine Dinge können uns entzücken,
Auch kleine Dinge können teuer sein.
Bedenkt, wie gern wir uns mit Perlen schmücken;
Sie werden schwer bezahlt und sind nur klein.
Bedenkt, wie klein ist die Olivenfrucht,
Und wird um ihre Güte doch gesucht.
Denkt an die Rose nur, wie klein sie ist,
Und duftet doch so lieblich, wie ihr wißt.

Paul Johann Ludwig Heyse, 1830–1914 (from the Italian)

Auf ein altes Bild

In grüner Landschaft Sommerflor,
Bei kühlem Wasser, Schilf und Rohr,
Schau, wie das Knäblein Sündelos
Frei spielet auf der Jungfrau Schoß!
Und dort im Walde wonnesam,
Ach, grünet schon des Kreuzes Stamm!

Eduard Friedrich Mörike, 1804–75

and decked with life? It is Anacreon's resting place.
Spring, summer, and autumn delighted the happy poet;
from the winter the mound at last has sheltered him.

Even Little Things

Even little things can delight us;
even little things can be precious.
Think with what pleasure we bedeck ourselves with pearls;
they are very costly, yet very small.
Think how small is the olive,
and yet sought after for its excellence.
Only think of the rose, how small it is,
and yet so fragrant, as you know.

On an Old Painting

In the green landscape, summer flowers;
by the cool water, rushes and reeds—
see how the innocent boy
plays happily upon the Virgin's lap!
And yonder in the pleasant wood,
ah! already the cross is growing.

Begegnung

Was doch heut Nacht ein Sturm gewesen,
Bis erst der Morgen sich geregt!
Wie hat der ungebetne Besen
Kamin und Gassen ausgefegt!

Da kommt ein Mädchen schon die Strassen,
Das halb verschüchtert um sich sieht;
Wie Rosen, die der Wind zerblasen,
So unstet ihr Gesichtchen glüht.

Ein schöner Bursch tritt ihr entgegen,
Er will ihr voll Entzücken nahn:
Wie sehn sich freudig und verlegen
Die ungewohnten Schelme an!

Er scheint zu fragen, ob das Liebchen
Die Zöpfe schon zurecht gemacht,
Die heute Nacht im offen Stübchen
Ein Sturm in Unordnung gebracht.

Der Bursche träumt noch von den Küssen,
Die ihm das süsse Kind getauscht,
Er steht, von Anmut hingerissen,
Derweil sie um die Ecke rauscht.

Eduard Friedrich Mörike, 1804–75

(Max Reger, op. 62, no. 13)

Beherzigung

Feiger Gedanken
Bängliches Schwanken,
Weibisches Zagen,

Meeting

But last night what a storm there was;
it was still raining until this morning!
Like a spontaneous broom
it has cleaned the chimneys and the streets!

Already a girl comes on the street,
on her way she timidly looks around.
Like roses blown apart by the wind
her mobile face glows.

A handsome boy walks across from her—
he wants to come near and show his charm;
happy and embarrassed she sees
the strange rogue.

He seems to ask if the darling
has yet put her hair in order
which last night in the open room
was disheveled by a storm.

The boy is still dreaming of the kisses
which the sweet child exchanged.
He stands enraptured by her charms
while she rushes around the corner.

Careful Consideration

Timid thoughts'
anxious vacillating,
womanish nervousness,

Ängstliches Klagen
Wendet kein Elend,
Macht dich nicht frei.

Allen Gewalten
Zum Trutz sich erhalten;
Nimmer sich beugen,
Kräftig sich zeigen,
Rufet die Arme
Der Götter herbei.

Johann Wolfgang von Goethe, 1749–1832

(Johann Friedrich Reichardt)

Bei einer Trauung

Vor lauter hochadligen Zeugen
Kopuliert man ihrer zwei;
Die Orgel hängt voll Geigen,
Der Himmel nicht, mein Treu!

Seht doch! sie weint ja greulich,
Er macht ein Gesicht abscheulich!
Denn leider freilich, freilich,
Keine Lieb ist nicht dabei.

Eduard Friedrich Mörike, 1804–75

Die Bekehrte

Bei dem Glanz der Abendröte
Ging ich still den Weg entlang,
Damon saß und blies die Flöte,

uneasy complaining
turn away no misery,
don't make you free.

All power
bravely defying,
never yielding,
showing oneself strong—
summons the arms
of the gods.

At a Wedding

Witnessed by the highest nobility,
the two are joined.
The organ proclaims their ecstasy,
but not heaven, on my word.
Just look! She is weeping miserably,
he is making a monstrous face!
For, I am sorry to say, frankly
there is no love in it.

The Neophyte

In the glow of sunset
I walked silently along the path.
Damon sat and played his flute,

Daß es von den Felsen klang,
So la la!

Und er zog mich zu sich nieder,
Küßte mich so hold, so süß.
Und ich sagte: Blase wieder!
Und der gute Junge blies,
So la la!

Meine Ruh ist nun verloren,
Meine Freude floh davon,
Und ich hör vor meinen Ohren
Immer nur den alten Ton,
So la la, le ralla!

Johann Wolfgang von Goethe, 1749–1832

*(Wenzel J. Tomaschek, op. 54, no. 3; Max Stange, op. 13, no. 1;
Nicolai Medtner, op. 18, no. 2)*

Blumengruss

Der Strauss, den ich gepflücket,
Grüsse dich vieltausendmal!
Ich habe mich oft gebücket,
Ach, wohl eintausendmal,
Und ihn ans Herz gedrücket
Wie hunderttausendmal!

Johann Wolfgang von Goethe, 1749–1832

so that the cliffs resounded,
so la, la!

And he drew me down to him,
kissed me so fondly, so sweetly,
and I said: "Play again!"
And the good boy played,
so la, la!

My peace is now lost;
my joy therefore is flown,
and I hear in my ears
still only the old strain,
so la, la, la ralla!

Flower Greeting

The bouquet that I have gathered
greets you a thousand times!
I have bent down
ah, fully a thousand times,
and I have pressed it to my heart
a hundred thousand times!

Dass doch gemalt all' deine Reize wären

Dass doch gemalt all' deine Reize wären,
Und dann der Heidenfürst das Bildnis fände.
Er würde dir ein gross Geschenk verehren,
Und legte seine Kron' in deine Hände.
Zum rechten Glauben müsste sich bekehren
Sein ganzes Reich bis an sein fernstes Ende.
Im ganzen Lande würd' es ausgeschrieben,
Christ soll' ein Jeder werden und dich lieben.
Ein jeder Heide flugs bekehrte sich
Und würd ein guter Christ und liebte dich.

Paul Johann Ludwig Heyse, 1830–1914 (from the Italian)

Denk es, O Seele!

Ein Tännlein grünet wo,
Wer weiß, im Walde,
Ein Rosenstrauch, wer sagt,
In welchem Garten?
Sie sind erlesen schon,
Denk es, o Seele!
Auf deinem Grab zu wurzeln
Und zu wachsen.

Zwei schwarze Rößlein weiden
Auf der Wiese,
Sie kehren heim zur Stadt
In muntern Sprüngen.
Sie werden schrittweis gehn
Mit deiner Leiche;
Vielleicht, vielleicht noch eh
An ihren Hufen

Would That All Your Charms Were Painted

Would that all your charms were painted,
and then that the heathen prince might find the portrait.
He would honor you with a great gift,
and lay his crown in your hands.
To the true faith must be converted
his whole kingdom to its remotest end.
Throughout the land it would be proclaimed:
Everyone must become a Christian and love you.
Each heathen straightway would be converted,
become a good Christian, and love you.

Think of It, O Soul!

A young fir is growing, where?—
who knows?—in the forest;
a rosebush, who can say
in what garden?
They are already chosen,
think of it, o soul,
upon your grave to root
and grow.

Two black colts are grazing
in the meadow;
they gambol
gaily back to town.
They will be pacing
with your body—
perhaps, perhaps before
their hoofs

Das Eisen los wird,
Das ich blitzen sehe!

Eduard Friedrich Mörike, 1804–75

(Robert Franz, op. 27, no. 6; Hans Pfitzner, op. 30, no. 3; Robert
Kahn, op. 12, no. 5; others)

Die ihr schwebet

Die ihr schwebet
Um diese Palmen
In Nacht und Wind,
Ihr heilgen Engel,
Stillet die Wipfel!
Es schlummert mein Kind.

Ihr Palmen von Bethlehem
Im Windesbrausen,
Wie mögt ihr heute
So zornig sausen!
O rauscht nicht also!
Schweiget, neiget
Euch leis und lind;
Stillet die Wipfel!
Es schlummert mein Kind.

Der Himmelsknabe
Duldet Beschwerde,
Ach, wie so müd er ward
Vom Leid der Erde.
Ach nun im Schlaf ihm
Leise gesänftigt
Die Qual zerrinnt,
Stillet die Wipfel!
Es schlummert mein Kind.

lose the shoes
that I see flashing!

Ye Hovering Angels

Ye who hover
about these palms
in the night and the wind,
ye holy angels,
quiet the treetops!
My child is asleep.

Ye palms of Bethlehem
in the blustering wind,
how can you today
howl so angrily?
O do not rustle so!
Be silent, bow down
softly and gently.
Quiet the treetops!
My child is asleep.

The Son of Heaven
must endure hardships;
ah, how weary He is
from the sorrow of the world.
Ah, now in sleep
quietly comforted,
His torment disappears.
Quiet the treetops!
My child is asleep.

Grimmige Kälte
Sauset hernieder,
Womit nur deck ich
Des Kindleins Glieder!
O all ihr Engel,
Die ihr geflügelt
Wandelt im Wind,
Stillet die Wipfel!
Es schlummert mein Kind.

Emanuel Geibel, 1815–84 (after Lope de Vega)

(Johannes Brahms, op. 97, no. 2)

Elfenlied

Bei Nacht im Dorf der Wächter rief: "Elfe!"
Ein ganz kleines Elfchen im Walde schlief—wohl um die Elfe!—
Und meint, es rief ihm aus dem Tal
Bei seinem Namen die Nachtigall,
Oder Silpelit hätt ihm gerufen.
Reibt sich der Elf die Augen aus,
Begibt sich vor sein Schneckenhaus
Und ist als wie ein trunken Mann,
Sein Schläflein war nicht voll getan,
Und humpelt also tippe tapp
Durchs Haselholz ins Tal hinab,
Schlupft an der Mauer hin so dicht,
Da sitzt der Glühwurm, Licht an Licht.
"Was sind das helle Fensterlein?
Da drin wird eine Hochzeit sein:
Die Kleinen sitzen beim Mahle
Und treiben's in dem Saale;
Da guck ich wohl ein wenig 'nein!"
—Pfui, stößt den Kopf an harten Stein!
Elfe, gelt, du hast genug?
Guckuck! Guckuck!

Eduard Friedrich Mörike, 1804–75

Bitter cold winds
rage on the earth.
How can I cover
my child's limbs?
O all ye angels
whose wings
bear you on the wind,
quiet the treetops!
My child is asleep.

Elf Song

At night in the village the watchman calls:
   "Eleven!"
A very small elf is asleep in the woods—
   at exactly eleven!—
and thinks that from the valley
the nightingale
is calling him by name,
or Silpelit has been calling him.
The elf rubs his eyes,
sets out from his snail house,
and is like a drunken man
not having finished his sleep,
and hobbles tippe tappe
down through the hazel wood to the valley,
slips along close to the wall
where the glowworms sit, light by light.
"What are those bright windows?
there must be a wedding in there:
the little ones sit at a banquet,
making merry in the hall.
I'll look in there a bit!"
Pfui! he bangs his head on the hard stone!
Elf, really have you had enough?
Cuckoo, cuckoo!

Epiphanias

Die heilgen drei König' mit ihrem Stern,
Sie essen, sie trinken, und bezahlen nicht gern;
Sie essen gern, sie trinken gern,
Sie essen, trinken, und bezahlen nicht gern.

Die heilgen drei König' sind kommen allhier,
Es sind ihrer drei und sind nicht ihrer vier;
Und wenn zu dreien der vierte wär,
So wär ein heilger drei König mehr.

Ich erster bin der weiß' und auch der schön',
Bei Tage solltet ihr erst mich sehn!
Doch ach, mit allen Spezerein
Werd ich sein Tag kein Mädchen mir erfrein.

Ich aber bin der braun' und bin der lang',
Bekannt bei Weibern wohl und bei Gesang.
Ich bringe Gold statt Spezerein,
Da werd ich überall willkommen sein.

Ich endlich bin der schwarz' und bin der klein'
Und mag auch wohl einmal recht lustig sein.
Ich esse gern, ich trinke gern,
Ich esse, trinke und bedanke mich gern.

Die heilgen drei König' sind wohlgesinnt,
Sie suchen die Mutter und das Kind;
Der Joseph fromm sitzt auch dabei,
Der Ochs und Esel liegen auf der Streu.

Wir bringen Myrrhen, wir bringen Gold,
Dem Weihrauch sind die Damen hold;
Und haben wir Wein von gutem Gewächs,
So trinken wir drei so gut als ihrer sechs.

Epiphany

The three holy kings with their star,
eat, drink, and don't like to pay;
they like to eat, they like to drink,
they eat, drink, and don't like to pay.

The three holy kings have come here—
there are three of them and not four—
and if to the three there were a fourth,
then there would be one holy king more.

I, the first, am the white and the handsome one,
you should just see me by day!
Yet ah, with all these spices
there will never be a day when I win a girl.

But I am the brown and the tall one,
well known to women and to song.
I bring gold instead of spices,
and so I will be welcome everywhere.

Lastly, I am the black and the little one,
and like to be merry.
I like to eat, I like to drink,
I eat, drink and like to say thank you.

The three holy kings are well disposed;
they seek the mother and the child.
Joseph too sits by,
the ox and the donkey lie on the straw.

We bring myrrh, we bring gold,
frankinsense that pleases the ladies,
and we have wine of good vintage,
so we three drink as well as six.

Da wir nun hier schöne Herrn und Fraun,
Aber keine Ochsen und Esel schaun,
So sind wir nicht am rechten Ort
Und ziehen unseres Weges weiter fort.

Johann Wolfgang von Goethe, 1749–1832

(Carl Friedrich Zelter)

Er ist's

Frühling läßt sein blaues Band
Wieder flattern durch die Lüfte;
Süße, wohlbekannte Düfte
Streifen ahnungsvoll das Land.
Veilchen träumen schon,
Wollen balde kommen.
Horch, von fern ein leiser Harfenton!
Frühling, ja du bist's!
Dich hab ich vernommen!

Eduard Friedrich Mörike, 1804–75

*(Robert Schumann, op. 79, no. 2; Robert Franz, op. 27, no. 2;
Eduard Lassen; Othmar Schoeck, op. 51, no. 4; others)*

Der Feuerreiter

Sehet ihr am Fensterlein
Dort die rote Mütze wieder?
Nicht geheuer muß es sein,
Denn er geht schon auf und nieder.
Und auf einmal welch Gewühle
Bei der Brücke, nach dem Feld!
Horch! das Feuerglöcklein gellt:

But now here, fine gentlemen and ladies,
we see no oxen or donkeys,
so we are not in the right place,
and will go further on our way.

It is He

Spring is floating his blue banner
once again on the breezes;
sweet, well-remembered fragrances
are portentously overrunning the land.
Violets, already dreaming,
will soon begin to bloom.
Listen! far off the soft sound of a harp!
Spring, it is you!
I have heard you!

The Fire-Rider

Do you see at the window
there, his red cap again?
There must be something wrong,
for he's pacing back and forth.
And suddenly, what a tumult
at the bridge and beyond the field!
Listen, the fire bell:

Hinterm Berg,
Hinterm Berg
Brennt es in der Mühle!

Schaut, da sprengt er wütend schier
Durch das Tor, der Feuerreiter,
Auf dem rippendürren Tier,
Als auf einer Feuerleiter!
Querfeldein. Durch Qualm und Schwüle
Rennt er schon und ist am Ort!
Drüben schallt es fort und fort:
Hinterm Berg,
Hinterm Berg
Brennt es in der Mühle!

Der so oft den roten Hahn
Meilenweit von fern gerochen,
Mit des heilgen Kreuzes Span
Freventlich die Glut besprochen—
Weh! dir grinst vom Dachgestühle
Dort der Feind im Höllenschein.
Gnade Gott der Seele dein!
Hinterm Berg,
Hinterm Berg
Rast er in der Mühle!

Keine Stunde hielt es an,
Bis die Mühle borst in Trümmer;
Doch den kecken Reitersmann
Sah man von der Stunde nimmer.
Volk und Wagen im Gewühle
Kehren heim von all dem Graus;
Auch das Glöcklein klinget aus:
Hinterm Berg,
Hinterm Berg
Brennt's!—

Nach der Zeit ein Müller fand

Beyond the mountain,
beyond the mountain
the mill is on fire.

Look! he is galloping almost crazy
through the gate, the fire-rider,
on his skinny animal,
as if on a fireman's ladder!
Cross-country! Through smoke and stifling heat,
he races and is there!
Over there it sounds on and on:
Beyond the mountain,
beyond the mountain
the mill is on fire.

You who so often have smelt fire
from miles away,
with a splinter of the true cross
wickedly have conjured the flames,
woe! Grinning at you from the rafters
there is the foe in the light of hell,
God have mercy on your soul!
Beyond the mountain,
beyond the mountain
he's raging in the mill!

It was not an hour
before the mill collapsed in ruins:
but the audacious horseman
was not seen from that hour.
People and wagons in tumult
return home from all the horror;
and the bell stops:
Beyond the mountain,
beyond the mountain
it's burning!—

Sometime after, a miller found

Ein Gerippe samt der Mützen
Aufrecht an der Kellerwand
Auf der beinern Mähre sitzen:
Feuerreiter, wie so kühle
Reitest du in deinem Grab!
Husch! da fällt's in Asche ab.
   Ruhe wohl,
   Ruhe wohl
Drunten in der Mühle!

Eduard Friedrich Mörike, 1804–75

Der Freund

Wer auf den Wogen schliefe,
Ein sanft gewiegtes Kind,
Kennt nicht des Lebens Tiefe,
Vor süßem Träumen blind.

Doch wen die Stürme fassen
Zu wildem Tanz und Fest,
Wen hoch auf dunklen Straßen
Die falsche Welt verläßt:

Der lernt sich wacker rühren,
Durch Nacht und Klippen hin
Lernt der das Steuer führen
Mit sichrem, ernstem Sinn.

Der ist vom echten Kerne,
Erprobt zu Lust und Pein,
Der glaubt an Gott und Sterne,
Der soll mein Schiffmann sein!

Joseph, Freiherr von Eichendorff, 1788–1857

(A. Püringer, op. 1, no. 2; Gabriella Wurzer)

a skeleton complete with cap,
erect against the cellar wall,
mounted on the gaunt mare.
Fire-rider, how cool
you ride in your grave!
Hush! It falls into ashes.
    Rest well,
    rest well
down there in the mill!

The Friend

He who sleeps on the waves
like a gently cradled child
does not know the depths of life—
blinded from sweet dreaming.

But he who is pressed by the storm
into wild dance and feasting,
whom, high on the dark sea-ways
the false world forsakes:

he learns to bestir himself bravely
forth through night and reefs,
learns to steer the rudder
securely and earnestly.

He is true in heart,
experienced in joy and pain,
he believes in God and the stars:
he shall be my pilot!

Fussreise

Am frischgeschnittnen Wanderstab,
Wenn ich in der Frühe
So durch die Wälder ziehe,
Hügel auf und ab:
Dann, wie's Vögelein im Laube
Singet und sich rührt,
Oder wie die goldne Traube
Wonnegeister spürt
In der ersten Morgensonne:
So fühlt auch mein alter, lieber
Adam Herbst- und Freühlingsfieber,
Gottbeherzte,
Nie verscherzte
Erstlings-Paradieseswonne.

Also bist du nicht so schlimm, o alter
Adam, wie die strengen Lehrer sagen;
Liebst und lobst du immer doch,
Singst und preisest immer noch,
Wie an ewig neuen Schöpfungstagen,
Deinen lieben Schöpfer und Erhalter.

Möcht es dieser geben,
Und mein ganzes Leben
Wär im leichten Wanderschweiße
Eine solche Morgenreise!

Eduard Friedrich Mörike, 1804–75

Der Gärtner

Auf ihrem Leibrößlein,
So weiß wie der Schnee,

Tramping

When with my fresh-cut walking stick
in the early morning
I press through the woods,
up hill and down hill,
then, as the bird in the branches
sings and moves about,
or as the golden cluster of grapes
feels the rapture
of the early morning sun,
so in me the old Adam
feels autumn and spring fever,
the God-given,
never forfeited
bliss of pristine paradise.
So you aren't such a sinner, old
Adam, as the straight-laced teachers say;
you still love and extol
and ever sing and praise—
as in the eternally new days of creation—
your dear Creator and Preserver!
O that it might be given me
that my whole life
could be, gently perspiring,
such a morning ramble!

The Gardener

On her favorite mount,
white as snow,

Die schönste Prinzessin
Reit't durch die Allee.

Der Weg, den das Rößlein
Hintanzet so hold,
Der Sand, den ich streute,
Er blinket wie Gold.

Du rosenfarbs Hütlein,
Wohl auf und wohl ab,
O wirf eine Feder
Verstohlen herab!

Und willst du dagegen
Eine Blüte von mir,
Nimm tausend für eine,
Nimm alle dafür!

Eduard Friedrich Mörike, 1804–75

(Robert Schumann, op. 107, no. 3; Robert Kahn, op. 16, no. 1;
Hermann Graedner)

Ganymed

Wie im Morgenglanze
Du rings mich anglühst,
Frühling, Geliebter!
Mit tausendfacher Liebeswonne
Sich an mein Herz drängt
Deiner ewigen Wärme
Heilig Gefühl,
Unendliche Schöne!

Daß ich dich fassen möcht
In diesen Arm!

the loveliest princess
rides through the avenue.

On the way where her little horse
gallops so charmingly,
the sand that I have strewn
sparkles like gold.

O little rose-colored hat,
moving up and down,
O throw a feather
stealthily down!

And if for that you want
a flower from me,
take a thousand for one,
take all for it!

Ganymede

In the splendor of the morning
how you glow about me,
spring, beloved!
with the thousand raptures of love
my heart is filled
by your eternal warmth's
hallowed emotion,
endless beauty!

O that I might hold you
in my arms!

Ach, an deinem Busen
Lieg ich, schmachte,
Und deine Blumen, dein Gras
Drängen sich an mein Herz.
Du kühlst den brennenden
Durst meines Busens,
Lieblicher Morgenwind!
Ruft drein die Nachtigall
Liebend nach mir aus dem Nebeltal.

Ich komm, ich komme!
Wohin? Ach, wohin?

Hinauf! Hinauf strebt's.
Es schweben die Wolken
Abwärts, die Wolken
Neigen sich der sehnenden Liebe.
Mir! Mir!
In euerm Schoße
Aufwärts!
Umfangend umfangen!
Aufwärts an deinen Busen,
Alliebender Vater!

Johann Wolfgang von Goethe, 1749–1832

*(Franz Schubert, D. 544; Carl Loewe, op. 81, no. 5; Johann
Friedrich Reichardt)*

Gebet

Herr! schicke was du willt,
Ein Liebes oder Leides;
Ich bin vergnügt, daß beides
Aus deinen Händen quillt.

Ah, on your bosom
I lie, languishing,
and your flowers, your grass,
press against my heart!
You cool the burning
thirst of my bosom,
lovely morning breeze.
The nightingale calls
lovingly to me from the misty valley.

I come, I come!
Whither, ah whither?

Upward, upward I soar.
The clouds float
down, the clouds
bend down with yearning love
to me! To me!
Into their lap,
upwards!
Embraced, embracing!
Upwards to Thy bosom
All-loving Father!

Prayer

Lord, send what Thou wilt,
good things or bad;
I am satisfied that both
come from Thy hands.

Wollest mit Freuden und wollest mit Leiden
Mich nicht überschütten!
Doch in der Mitten
Liegt holdes Bescheiden.

Eduard Friedrich Mörike, 1804–75

(Felix Weingartner, op. 44, no. 2; Richard Trunk; Louis Victor
Saar, op. 54, no. 2; many others)

Der Genesene an die Hoffnung

Tödlich graute mir der Morgen:
Doch schon lag mein Haupt, wie süß!
Hoffnung, dir im Schoß verborgen,
Bis der Sieg gewonnen hieß.
Opfer bracht ich allen Göttern,
Doch vergessen warest du;
Seitwärts von den ewgen Rettern
Sahest du dem Feste zu.

O vergib, du Vielgetreue!
Tritt aus deinem Dämmerlicht,
Daß ich dir ins ewig neue,
Mondenhelle Angesicht
Einmal schaue, recht von Herzen,
Wie ein Kind und sonder Harm;
Ach, nur einmal ohne Schmerzen
Schließe mich in deinen Arm!

Eduard Friedrich Mörike, 1804–75

Gesang des Harfners I

Wer sich der Einsamkeit ergibt,
Ach! der ist bald allein;

Neither with happiness
nor with affliction
do Thou overwhelm me!
For in between
lies gentle moderation.

The Convalescent to Hope

Fatefully the day dawned for me,
yet, how sweetly my head now lay,
hope, hidden on your lap
until the victory was won.
I made offerings to all the gods,
but you were forgotten;
set apart from the eternal redeemers,
you looked upon the feast.

O forgive, faithful one!
Come forth from your twilight
that I may ever look anew
upon your moonbright face
for once from my very heart;
like a child and free from sorrow,
ah, only once without pain
draw me in your arms!

Song of the Harper I

He who gives himself to solitude,
ah, he is soon alone;

Ein jeder lebt, ein jeder liebt,
Und läßt ihn seiner Pein.

Ja! laßt mich meiner Qual!
Und kann ich nur einmal
Recht einsam sein,
Dann bin ich nicht allein.

Es schleicht ein Liebender lauschend sacht,
Ob seine Freundin allein?
So überschleicht bei Tag und Nacht
Mich Einsamen die Pein,

Mich Einsamen die Qual.
Ach werd ich erst einmal
Einsam im Grabe sein,
Da läßt sie mich allein!

Johann Wolfgang von Goethe, 1749–1832

(Franz Schubert, D. 478; Robert Schumann, op. 98a, no. 6;
Anton Rubinstein, op. 91, no. 2; many others)

Gesang des Harfners II

An die Türen will ich schleichen,
Still und sittsam will ich stehn,
Fromme Hand wird Nahrung reichen,
Und ich werde weiter gehn.
Jeder wird sich glücklich scheinen,
Wenn mein Bild vor ihm erscheint,
Eine Träne wird er weinen,
Und ich weiß nicht, was er weint.

Johann Wolfgang von Goethe, 1749–1832

(Franz Schubert, D. 479; Johann Friedrich Reichardt; Anton
Rubinstein, op. 91, no. 9; Nicolai Medtner, op. 15, no. 2; Robert
Schmann, op. 98a, no. 8; many others)

others live, others love,
and leave him to his torment.

Yes, leave me my affliction!
And if I can only once
be really lonely,
then I am not alone.

A lover steals softly and listens—
is his beloved alone?
So day and night
I the lonely one am stalked by pain.

I the lonely one am stalked by torment.
Ah, once I am
lonely in the grave,
they will leave me alone!

Song of the Harper II

I will steal to the doors;
quiet and humble will I stand.
An honest hand will offer me food,
and I will go away.
Everyone will consider himself fortunate,
when my form appears to him;
one tear will be shed,
and I know not why he weeps.

Gesang des Harfners III

Wer nie sein Brot mit Tränen aß,
Wer nie die kummervollen Nächte
Auf seinem Bette weinend saß,
Der kennt euch nicht, ihr himmlischen Mächte.

Ihr führt ins Leben uns hinein,
Ihr laßt den Armen schuldig werden,
Dann überlaßt ihr ihn der Pein;
Denn alle Schuld rächt sich auf Erden.

Johann Wolfgang von Goethe, 1749–1832

(Franz Schubert, D. 480; Robert Schumann, op. 98, no. 4; Carl Friedrich Zelter; Anton Rubinstein, op. 91, no. 2; many others)

Gesang Weylas

Du bist Orplid, mein Land!
Das ferne leuchtet;
Vom Meere dampfet dein besonnter Strand
Den Nebel, so der Götter Wange feuchtet.

Uralte Wasser steigen
Verjüngt um deine Hüften, Kind!
Vor deiner Gottheit beugen
Sich Könige, die deine Wärter sind.

Eduard Friedrich Mörike, 1804–75

(Max Lewandowsky)

Song of the Harper III

He who has never eaten his bread with tears,
who never sat through sorrowful nights
weeping on his bed,
he knows you not, ye heavenly powers!

You bring us into life;
you let the poor man go astray,
then leave him to his torture,
for every sin avenges itself upon thie earth!

Weyla's Song

Thou art Orplid, my land
that shinest afar;
from the sea thy sunny shore exhales
the mist to moisten the cheeks of the gods.

Timeless waters rise
renewed about thy slopes, child!
Before thy godhead bow
kings, who are thy guardians.

Grenzen der Menschheit

Wenn der uralte,
Heilige Vater
Mit gelassener Hand
Aus rollenden Wolken
Segnende Blitze
Über die Erde sät,
Küß ich den letzten
Saum seines Kleides,
Kindliche Schauer
Treu in der Brust.

Denn mit Göttern
Soll sich nicht messen
Irgendein Mensch.
Hebt er sich aufwärts
Und berührt
Mit dem Scheitel die Sterne,
Nirgends haften dann
Die unsichern Sohlen,
Und mit ihm spielen
Wolken und Winde.

Steht er mit festen,
Markigen Knochen
Auf der wohlbegründeten
Dauernden Erde,
Reicht er nicht auf,
Nur mit der Eiche
Oder der Rebe
Sich zu vergleichen.

Was unterscheidet
Götter von Menschen?
Daß viele Welten
Vor jenen wandeln,

Human Limitations

When the ancient
holy father
with imperturbable hand
from rolling clouds
sows blessed lightnings
over the earth,
I kiss the last
hem of his garment
with childlike awe
in my faithful breast.

For against the gods
no mortal
should measure himself.
If he raises himself up
and reaches
the stars with the top of his head,
nowhere will he find
a secure foothold,
and with him
clouds and wind make sport.

If he stands with firm
healthy bones
on the well grounded
enduring earth,
he does not reach up
even as high as the oak,
nor with the vine
can he compare.

What is the difference
between gods and mortals?
That many waves
roll before them,

Ein ewiger Strom:
Uns hebt die Welle,
Und wir versinken.

Ein kleiner Ring
Begrenzt unser Leben,
Und viele Geschlechter
Reihen sich dauernd
An ihres Daseins
Unendliche Kette.

Johann Wolfgang von Goethe, 1749–1832

(Franz Schubert, D. 716; Alban Berg, op. 3; J. Kohler; others)

Heimweh

Wer in die Fremde will wandern,
Der muß mit der Liebsten gehn,
Es jubeln und lassen die andern
Den Fremden alleine stehn.

Was wisset ihr, dunkele Gipfel,
Von der alten, schönen Zeit?
Ach, die heimat hinter den Gipfeln,
Wie liegt sie von hier so weit.

Am liebsten betracht ich die Sterne,
Die schienen, wie ich ging zu ihr,
Die Nachtigall hör ich so gerne,
Sie sang vor der Liebsten Tür.

Der Morgen, das ist meine Freude!
Da steig ich in stiller Stund
Auf den höchsten Berg in die Weite,
Grüß dich, Deutschland, aus Herzensgrund!

Joseph, Freiherr von Eichendorff, 1788–1857

an eternal stream:
the waves lift us,
the waves engulf us,
and we are submerged.

A small ring
limits our life,
and many generations
are endlessly linked
in their existence's
endless chain.

Homesickness

He who would travel abroad
must go with his beloved;
others make merry and leave
the stranger alone.

What do you know, dark mountaintops,
of the old, happy times?
Ah, the homeland beyond the mountains,
how far it is from here.

I prefer to watch the stars
that shone when I went to her,
I so love to hear the nightingale
that sang before my beloved's door.

The morning is my delight!
Then I climb in the quiet time;
on the highest mountain, in the distance
I greet you, Germany, from the bottom of my heart!

In dem Schatten meiner Locken

In dem Schatten meiner Locken
Schlief mir mein Geliebter ein.
Weck ich ihn nun auf?—Ach nein!

Sorglich strählt ich meine krausen
Locken täglich in der Frühe,
Doch umsonst ist meine Mühe,
Weil die Winde sie zersausen.
Lockenschatten, Windessausen
Schläferten den Liebsten ein.
Weck ich ihn nun auf?—Ach nein!

Hören muβ ich, wie ihn gräme,
Daβ er schmachtet schon so lange,
Daβ ihm Leben geb und nehme
Diese meine braune Wange,
Und er nennt mich seine Schlange,
Und doch schlief er bei mir ein.
Weck ich ihn nun auf?—Ach nein!

Paul Johann Ludwig Heyse, 1830–1914 (from the Spanish)

(Johannes Brahms, op. 6, no. 1; Adolf Jensen, op. 1, no. 4; Max
Mayer, op. 14; Emil Sjögren)

In der Frühe

Kein Schlaf noch kühlt das Auge mir,
Dort gehet schon der Tag herfür
An meinem Kammerfenster.
Es wühlet mein verstörter Sinn
Noch zwischen Zweifeln her und hin
Und schaffet Nachtgespenster.
—Ängste, quäle

In the Shadow of My Curls

In the shadow of my curls
my lover lies asleep.
Shall I wake him? Ah, no!

Carefully I have combed my curly
locks every morning,
but my trouble is in vain,
because the winds dishevel them.
Shadow of curls, rush of wind,
put my lover to sleep.
Shall I wake him? Ah, no!

I must listen to his complaining
that he languished so long,
that his whole life depends
on these brown cheeks of mine.
And he calls me his serpent,
and yet he sleeps beside me.
Shall I wake him? Ah, no!

Early Morning

Still no sleep cools my eyes;
the day is already beginning to dawn
there at my bedroom window.
My troubled spirit is still tossed about
between one doubt and another,
and raises phantoms.
Be not worried, torment yourself

Dich nicht länger, meine Seele!
Freu dich! Schon sind da und dorten
Morgenglocken wach geworden.

Eduard Friedrich Mörike, 1804–75

*(Max Reger; Max Stange; Siegmund von Hausegger; Pauline
Viardot-Garcia; others)*

Lied der Mignon I

Heiß mich nicht reden, heiß mich schweigen,
Denn mein Geheimnis ist mir Pflicht;
Ich möchte dir mein ganzes Innre zeigen,
Allein das Schicksal will es nicht.

Zur rechten Zeit vertreibt der Sonne Lauf
Die finstre Nacht, und sie muß sich erhellen,
Der harte Fels schließt seinen Busen auf,
Mißgönnt der Erde nicht die tiefverborgnen Quellen.

Ein jeder sucht im Arm des Freundes Ruh,
Dort kann die Brust in Klagen sich ergießen;
Allein ein Schwur drückt mir die Lippen zu,
Und nur ein Gott vermag sie aufzuschließen.

Johann Wolfgang von Goethe, 1749–1832

*(Franz Schubert, D. 877; Robert Schumann, op. 98a, no. 5;
Johann Friedrich Reichardt; Carl Friedrich Zelter; Anton
Rubinstein, op. 91, no. 10; others)*

no longer, my soul!
Rejoice! Already here and there
morning bells have awakened.

Mignon's Song I

Do not ask me to speak, tell me to be silent,
for my secret is my duty;
I would reveal to you my inmost being,
but fate will not have it so.

At the appointed hour the sun's course drives away
the gloomy night, and it cannot choose but brighten.
The hard rock opens its bosom;
it does not begrudge the earth its deep-hidden springs.

Everyone seeks rest in the arms of a friend,
for there he can pour out the troubles of his heart.
But a vow seals my lips,
and only a god can prevail upon me to open them.

Lied der Mignon II

Nur wer die Sehnsucht kennt,
Weiß, was ich leide!
Allein und abgetrennt
Von aller Freude,
Seh ich ans Firmament
Nach jener Seite.
Ach! der mich liebt und kennt,
Ist in der Weite.
Es schwindelt mir, es brennt
Mein Eingeweide.
Nur wer die Sehnsucht kennt,
Weiß, was ich leide!

Johann Wolfgang von Goethe, 1749–1832

*(Franz Schubert, D. 359, 877, 310; Robert Schumann, op. 98a,
no. 3; Piotr Illich Tchaikovski, op. 6, no. 6; Carl Loewe, op. 9;
Nicolai Medtner, op. 18, no. 4; many more)*

Lied der Mignon III

So laßt mich scheinen, bis ich werde;
Zieht mir das weiße Kleid nicht aus!
Ich eile von der schönen Erde
Hinab in jenes feste Haus.

Dort ruh ich eine kleine Stille,
Dann öffnet sich der frische Blick,
Ich lasse dann die reine Hülle,
Den Gürtel und den Kranz zurück.

Und jene himmlischen Gestalten,
Sie fragen nicht nach Mann und Weib,

Mignon's Song II

Only one who knows longing
can understand what I suffer!
Alone and bereft
of all joy,
I look at the sky
yonder.
Ah, he who loves and understands me
is far away.
I faint. Fire burns
within me.
Only one who knows longing
can understand what I suffer!

Mignon's Song III

So let me seem, until I become so;
do not divest me of my white garment!
I am hastening from the beautiful earth
down to that impregnable house.

There I shall rest awhile in tranquility,
then a fresh vision will open up.
I shall then leave behind the pure raiment,
the girdle and the wreath.

And those heavenly beings
do not concern themselves with man and woman,

Und keine Kleider, keine Falten
Umgeben den verklärten Leib.

Zwar lebt ich ohne Sorg und Mühe,
Doch fühlt ich tiefen Schmerz genung;
Vor Kummer altert ich zu frühe;
Macht mich auf ewig wieder jung!

Johann Wolfgang von Goethe, 1749–1832

*(Franz Schubert, D. 469, 727, 877; Robert Schumann, op. 98a,
no. 9; Johann Friedrich Reichardt; others)*

Mignon

Kennst du das Land, wo die Zitronen blühn,
Im dunkeln Laub die Gold-Orangen glühn,
Ein sanfter Wind vom blauen Himmel weht,
Die Myrte still und hoch der Lorbeer steht?
Kennst du es wohl?—Dahin! Dahin!
Möcht' ich mit dir, o mein Geliebter, ziehn.

Kennst du das Haus? Auf Säulen ruht sein Dach,
Es glänzt der Saal, es schimmert das Gemach,
Und Marmorbilder stehn und sehn mich an:
Was hat man dir, du armes Kind, getan?
Kennst du es wohl?—Dahin! Dahin!
Möcht' ich mit dir, o mein Beschützer, ziehn.

Kennst du den Berg und seinen Wolkensteg?
Das Maultier sucht im Nebel seinen Weg;
In Höhlen wohnt der Drachen alte Brut;
Es stürzt der Fels und über ihn die Flut.
Kennst du es wohl?—Dahin! Dahin!
Geht unser Weg! o Vater, lass uns ziehn!

Johann Wolfgang von Goethe, 1749–1832

*(Ludwig van Beethoven, op. 75, no. 1; Robert Schumann, op.
98a, no. 1; Franz Schubert, D. 321; Franz Liszt; many others)*

and no garments, no robes,
cover the transfigured body.

True, I have lived without trouble and toil,
yet I have felt deep pain enough.
Through sorrow I have aged too early—
O make me forever young again!

Mignon

Do you know the country where the lemon trees bloom,
where among the dark leaves the golden oranges glow,
where a soft wind wafts from the blue heaven,
where the myrtle stands motionless and the laurel grows high?
Do you really know it?—There! There!
I would go with you, my beloved.

Do you know the house? Its roof rests on columns;
the great hall shines, the rooms glitter,
and marble statues stand looking at me—
"What have they done to you, poor child?"
Do you really know it?—There! There!
I would go with you, my protector.

Do you know the mountain and its cloud-veiled path?
The mule tries to find its way in the mist;
in the caves lives the ancient brood of dragons;
the cliff falls sheer and over it the torrent.
Do you really know it?—There! There!
leads our way! O father, let us go!

Morgenstimmung

Bald ist der Nacht ein End' gemacht,
Schon fühl' ich Morgenlüfte wehen.
Der Herr, der spricht: Es werde Licht!
Da muß, was dunkel ist, vergehen.
Vom Himmelszelt durch alle Welt
Die Engel freudejauchzend fliegen:
Der Sonne Strahl durchflammt das All.
Herr, laß uns kämpfen, laß uns siegen!

Robert Reinick, 1805–52

(Sir George Henschel, op. 46, no. 4)

Der Musikant

Wandern lieb ich für mein Leben,
Lebe eben, wie ich kann,
Wollt ich mir auch Mühe geben,
Paßt es mir doch gar nicht an.

Schöne alte Lieder weiß ich,
In der Kälte, ohne Schuh
Draußen in die Saiten reiß ich,
Weiß nicht, wo ich abends ruh.

Manche Schöne macht wohl Augen,
Meinet, ich gefiel ihr sehr,
Wenn ich nur was wollte taugen,
So ein armer Lump nicht wär.

Mag dir Gott ein' Mann bescheren,
Wohl mit Haus und Hof versehn!
Wenn wir zwei zusammen wären,
Möcht mein Singen mir vergehn.

Joseph, Freiherr von Eichendorff, 1788–1857

Morning Mood

Soon night will end;
already I feel the morning breezes stirring.
The Lord speaks: Let there by light!
Then must all darkness vanish.
From the vault of heaven through all the world
the angels fly rejoicing;
the beams of the sun flame through the universe.
Lord, let us battle, let us conquer!

The Musician

I love a wandering life;
I live any way I can.
I might worry about it,
but that sort of thing doesn't suit me.

I know beautiful old songs,
out in the cold, barefoot.
Outdoors I pluck the strings,
but I don't know where I'll rest at night.

Many a beauty makes eyes at me,
as if to tell me I please her—
if only I amounted to something,
and weren't such a poor good-for-nothing.

May God send you a man
well provided wth house and home!
If we two were to be together
I would forget how to sing.

Nimmersatte Liebe

So ist die Lieb! So ist die Lieb!
Mit Küssen nicht zu stillen:
Wer ist der Tor und will ein Sieb
Mit eitel Wasser füllen?

Und schöpfst du an die tausend Jahr
Und küssest ewig, ewig gar,
Du tust ihr nie zu Willen.
Die Lieb, die Lieb hat alle Stund
Neu wunderlich Gelüsten;
Wir bissen uns die Lippen wund,
Da wir uns heute küßten.
Das Mädchen hielt in guter Ruh,
Wie's Lämmlein unterm Messer;
Ihr Auge bat: "Nur immer zu!
Je weher, desto besser!"

So ist die Lieb! und war auch so,
Wie lang es Liebe gibt,
Und anders war Herr Salomo,
Der Weise, nicht verliebt.

Eduard Friedrich Mörike, 1804–75

(Eugen d'Albert; Max Vogrich)

Nun wandre, Maria
(Der heilige Joseph singt)

Nun wandre, Maria,
Nun wandre nur fort.
Schon krähen die Hähne,
Und nah ist der Ort.

Insatiable Love

Such is love, such is love,
not to be quieted with kisses:
who is such a fool as to fill a sieve
with water?
And were you to work a thousand years,
always, always kissing,
you could never satisfy her.

Love, love has every hour
some wonderful new desire.
We bit our lips sore
today when we were kissing.
The girl takes it calmly,
like a lamb under the knife.
Her eyes have led him on: so go ahead,
the more painful the better!

Such is love, and was indeed so
as long as love has existed;
and Lord Solomon himself, the sage,
did not love any other way.

Now Come Along, Mary
(Saint Joseph Sings)

Now come along, Mary,
keep on.
Already the cocks are crowing
and we are nearly there.

Nun wandre, Geliebte,
Du Kleinod mein,
Und balde wir werden
In Bethlehem sein.
Dann ruhest du fein
Und schlummerst dort.
Schon krähen die Hähne
Und nah ist der Ort.

Wohl seh ich, Herrin,
Die Kraft dir schwinden;
Kann deine Schmerzen,
Ach, kaum verwinden.
Getrost! Wohl finden
Wir Herberg dort.
Schon krähen die Hähne
Und nah ist der Ort

Wär erst bestanden
Dein Stündlein, Marie,
Die gute Botschaft,
Gut lohnt ich sie.
Das Eselein hie
Gäb ich drum fort!
Schon krähen die Hähne,
Komm! Nah ist der Ort.

Paul Johann Ludwig Heyse, 1830–1914 (from the Spanish)

(Max Bruch, op. 71; Adolf Jensen, op. 64, no. 1; Gustav Flügel,
op. 43, no. 1)

Prometheus

Bedecke deinen Himmel, Zeus,
Mit Wolkendunst
Und übe, dem Knaben gleich,

Now come along, beloved,
my jewel,
and soon we shall be
in Bethlehem.
Then you shall have a good rest
and sleep there.
Already the cocks are crowing
and we are nearly there.

I see very well, my lady,
that your strength is failing;
I can hardly bear
your pain any longer.
Courage! Surely we shall find
shelter there.
Already the cocks are crowing
and we are nearly there.

If only your time
were come, Mary,
the good news—
what would I give for it!
The donkey here,
I would part with him!
Already the cocks are crowing,
come! we are nearly there.

Prometheus

Cover your heavens, Zeus,
with misty clouds,
and play like a boy

Der Disteln köpft,
An Eichen dich und Bergeshöhn;
Mußt mir meine Erde
Doch lassen stehn
Und meine Hütte, die du nicht gebaut,
Und meinen Herd,
Um dessen Glut
Du mich beneidest.

Ich kenne nichts Ärmeres
Unter der Sonn als euch, Götter!
Ihr nährt kümmerlich
Von Opfersteuern
Und Gebetshauch
Eure Majestät
Und darbtet, wären
Nicht Kinder und Bettler
Hoffnungsvolle Toren.

Da ich ein Kind war,
Nicht wußte, wo aus noch ein,
Kehrt ich mein verirrtes Auge
Zur Sonne, als wenn drüber wär
Ein Ohr, zu hören meine Klage,
Ein Herz wie meins,
Sich des Bedrängten zu erbarmen.

Wer half mir
Wider der Titanen Übermut?
Wer rettete vom Tode mich,
Von Sklaverei?
Hast du nicht alles selbst vollendet,
Heilig glühend Herz?
Und glühtest jung und gut,
Betrogen, Rettungsdank
Dem Schlafenden da droben?

Ich dich ehren? Wofür?
Hast du die Schmerzen gelindert

who pulls the heads off thistles
with oaks and mountaintops!
But my earth
you must leave alone,
and my hut, which you did not build,
and my hearth, whose fire
you envy.

I know nothing more wretched
under the sun, than you gods!
You nourish miserably—
on required sacrifices
and the breath of prayer—
your majesty,
and you would starve if
children and beggars
were not hopeful fools.

When I was a child
and did not know out from in,
I would turn my wandering eyes
to the sun, as if above there were
an ear to hear my lament,
a heart like mine
to take pity on the distressed.

Who helped me
against the arrogance of the Titans?
Who delivered me from death,
from slavery?
Have you not done it all yourself,
glowing, dedicated heart?
And with fine youthful ardor
were you not betrayed into thanks for your delivery
to the sleeping one above?

I honor you? What for?
Have you ever soothed the affliction
of the heavy-laden?

Je des Beladenen?
Hast du die Tränen gestillet
Je des Geängstigten?
Hat nicht mich zum Manne geschmiedet
Die allmächtige Zeit
Und das ewige Schicksal,
Meine Herrn und deine?

Wähntest du etwa,
Ich sollte das Leben hassen,
In Wüsten fliehen,
Weil nicht alle
Blütenträume reiften?

Hier sitz ich, forme Menschen
Nach meinem Bilde,
Ein Geschlecht, das mir gleich sei,
Zu leiden, zu weinen,
Zu genießen und zu freuen sich,
Und dein nicht zu achten,
Wie ich!

Johann Wolfgang von Goethe, 1749–1832

(Franz Schubert, D. 674; Johann Friedrich Reichardt Julius Röntgen, op. 99)

Der Rattenfänger

Ich bin der wohlbekannte Sänger,
Der vielgereiste Rattenfänger,
Den diese altberühmte Stadt
Gewiß besonders nötig hat.
Und wärens Ratten noch so viele,
Und wären Wiesel mit im Spiele,
Von allen säubr ich diesen Ort,
Sie müssen miteinander fort.

Have you ever stilled the tears
of the distressed?
Was I not forged into manhood
by omnipotent time
and eternal destiny,
my masters and yours?

Do you perhaps imagine
that I ought to hate life,
and fly into the desert
because not all
flowery dreams come true?

Here I sit fashioning men
in my own image,
as a species like myself
to suffer, to weep,
to enjoy and to rejoice,
and to ignore you,
even as I!

The Rat Catcher

I am the well-known singer,
the much-traveled rat catcher,
of whom this fine old city
certainly has special need.
And were there ever so many rats,
and were there weasels playing with them,
I'll clear this place of them;
they must all go out together.

Dann ist der gut gelaunte Sänger
Mitunter auch ein Kinderfänger,
Der selbst die wildesten bezwingt,
Wenn er die goldnen Märchen singt.
Und wären Knaben noch so trutzig,
Und wären Mädchen noch so stutzig,
In meine Saiten greif ich ein,
Sie müssen alle hinterdrein.

Dann ist der vielgewandte Sänger
Gelegentlich ein Mädchenfänger;
In keinem Städtchen langt er an,
Wo ers nicht mancher angetan.
Und wären Mädchen noch so blöde,
Und wären Weiber noch so spröde,
Doch allen wird so liebebang
Bei Zaubersaiten und Gesang.

Johann Wolfgang von Goethe, 1749–1832

(Franz Schubert, D. 255)

Schlafendes Jesuskind

Sohn der Jungfrau, Himmelskind! am Boden
Auf dem Holz der Schmerzen eingeschlafen,
Das der fromme Meister, sinnvoll spielend,
Deinen leichten Träumen unterlegte;
Blume du, noch in der Knospe dämmernd
Eingehüllt die Herrlichkeit des Vaters!

O wer sehen könnte, welche Bilder
Hinter dieser Stirne, diesen schwarzen
Wimpern sich in sanftem Wechsel malen!

Eduard Friedrich Mörike, 1804–75

Moreover this good natured singer
is sometimes also a children-catcher,
who subdues even the most unruly
when he sings golden fairy tales.
And however defiant the boys,
and however startled the girls,
I strike my strings
and they all follow.

Also this versatile singer
is sometimes a girl-catcher;
in no town does he arrive
without captivating many.
And were girls ever so shy,
and were wives ever so prudish,
they all become lovelorn
at my magic strings and song.

Sleeping Christchild

Son of the Virgin, Heavenly Child! On the ground
asleep upon the wood of torture,
which the pious master, in a profound allegory,
laid under your peaceful dreams.
O flower, still in the bud, forebodingly
shrouded in the Father's glory!
O who could perceive what images
behind this brow, these black
eyelashes, are reflected in gentle succession!

Das Ständchen

Auf die Dächer zwischen blassen
Wolken schaut der Mond herfür,
Ein Student dort auf den Gassen
Singt vor seiner Liebsten Tür.

Und die Brunnen rauschen wieder
Durch die stille Einsamkeit,
Und der Wald vom Berge nieder,
Wie in alter, schöner Zeit.

So in meinen jungen Tagen
Hab ich manche Sommernacht
Auch die Laute hier geschlagen
Und manch lust'ges Lied erdacht.

Aber von der stillen Schwelle
Trugen sie mein Lieb zur Ruh,
Und du, fröhlicher Geselle,
Singe, sing nur immer zu!

Joseph, Freiherr von Eichendorff, 1789–1857

(Eduard Lassen; Erich Wolfgang Korngold, op. 9, no. 3; L.
Marschall, op. 10, no. 2; others)

Storchenbotschaft

Des Schäfers sein Haus und das steht auf zwei Rad,
Steht hoch auf der Heiden, so frühe wie spat;
Und wenn nur ein Mancher so'n Nachtquartier hätt!
Ein Schäfer tauscht nicht mit dem König sein Bett.
Und käm ihm zur Nacht auch was Seltsames vor,
Er betet sein Sprüchel und legt sich aufs Ohr;
Ein Geistlein, ein Hexlein, so luftige Wicht',

The Serenade

Over the roofs amid pale
clouds the moon shines through.
A student, there on the street,
is singing in front of his sweetheart's door.

And the fountains are splashing again
in the silent solitude,
and down from the woods on the mountain,
as in the old happier times.

So in my young days
many summer nights
I played my lute here
and made up many happy songs.

But from the silent threshold
they carried my love to rest.
And you, happy comrade,
sing on, only sing on forever.

The Storks' Message

The shepherd's house stands on two wheels,
stands high in the heath, early and late.
Many would be glad to have such a sleeping place.
A shepherd wouldn't change his bed with the king;
and if in the night anything unusual happened,
he would say a brief prayer and lie down.
A little ghost, a little witch, such an airy creature,

Sie klopfen ihm wohl, doch er antwortet nicht.
Einmal doch, da ward es ihm wirklich zu bunt:
Es knopert am Laden, es winselt der Hund;
Nun ziehet mein Schäfer den Riegel—ei schau!
Da stehen zwei Störche, der Mann und die Frau.
Das Pärchen, es machet ein schön Kompliment,
Es möchte gern reden, ach, wenn es nur könnt!

Was will mir das Ziefer? Ist sowas erhört?
Doch ist mir wohl fröhliche Botschaft beschert.
Ihr seid wohl dahinten zu Hause am Rhein?
Ihr habt wohl mein Mädel gebissen ins Bein?
Nun weinet das Kind und die Mutter noch mehr,
Sie wünschet den Herzallerliebsten sich her.
Und wünschet daneben die Taufe bestellt:
Ein Lämmlein, ein Würstlein, ein Beutelein Geld?
So sagt nur, ich käm' in zwei Tag oder drei,
Und grüßt mir mein Bübel und rührt ihm den Brei!
Doch halt! Warum stellt ihr zu Zweien euch ein?
Es werden doch, hoff' ich, nicht Zwillinge sein?
Da klappern die Störche im lustigsten Ton,
Sie nicken und knixen und fliegen davon.

Eduard Friedrich Mörike, 1804–75

Der Tambour

Wenn meine Mutter hexen könnt,
Da müßt sie mit dem Regiment
Nach Frankreich, überall mit hin,
Und wär die Marketenderin.
Im Lager, wohl um Mitternacht,
Wenn niemand auf ist als die Wacht
Und alles schnarchet, Roß und Mann,
Vor meiner Trommel säß ich dann:
Die Trommel müßt eine Schüssel sein,

may well come knocking, but he doesn't answer.
But once it was really too much:
knocking at the window, moaning of the dog;
now my shepherd unlocks, and behold!
There stand two storks, male and female.
The pair make a beautiful greeting:
they wanted to speak, only they couldn't!

What do they want of me? Whoever heard of such a thing?
Yet it must be good news for me.
Do you live over there on the Rhein?
Have you pecked my girl on the leg?
Now the child is crying and the mother even more;
she wishes her beloved were here.
And she wants also to arrange for the christening:
a little lamb, a sausage, a little purse of money?
Tell her I'll be coming in two or three days,
and greet my little boy and stir his pudding.
But hold! Why are there two of you standing there?
It wouldn't, I hope, be twins?
Then the storks clapped with a happy noise;
they nod and curtsy and fly away.

The Drummer Boy

If my mother could work magic,
then she would have to go with the regiment
to France, and elsewhere,
and she would be the camp-follower.
In camp at midnight,
when only the guard is up,
and everyone is snoring, horse and man,
then I would sit by my drum.
My drum would have to be a bowl

Ein warmes Sauerkraut darein,
Die Schlegel Messer und Gabel,
Eine lange Wurst mein Sabel;
Mein Tschako wär ein Humpen gut,
Den füll ich mit Burgunderblut.
Und weil es mir an Lichte fehlt,
Da scheint der Mond in mein Gezelt;
Scheint er auch auf französisch herein,
Mir fällt doch meine Liebste ein:
Ach weh! jetzt hat der Spaß ein End!
—Wenn nur meine Mutter hexen könnt!

Eduard Friedrich Mörike, 1804–75

Um Mitternacht

Gelassen stieg die Nacht ans Land,
Lehnt träumend an der Berge Wand,
Ihr Auge sieht die goldne Wage nun
Der Zeit in gleichen Schalen stille ruhn;
   Und kecker rauschen die Quellen hervor,
   Sie singen der Mutter, der Nacht, ins Ohr
   Vom Tage,
Vom heute gewesenen Tage.

Das uralt alte Schlummerlied,
Sie achtet's nicht, sie ist es müd;
Ihr klingt des Himmels Bläue süßer noch,
Der flüchtgen Stunden gleichgeschwungnes Joch.
   Doch immer behalten die Quellen das Wort,
   Es singen die Wasser im Schlafe noch fort
   Vom Tage.
Vom heute gewesenen Tage.

Eduard Friedrich Mörike, 1804–75

(Max Bruch, op. 59, no. 1; Robert Franz, op. 28, no. 6;
Ferdinand Hiller, op. 100)

with warm sauerkraut in it;
the drumsticks would be knife and fork,
my sabre a long sausage.
My shako would be a good tankard
which I would fill with Burgundy blood.
And since I lack a light
the moon shines into my tent.
It would also shine on the French.
I miss my sweetheart!
Oh dear, now the fun is over!
—if only my mother could work magic!

At Midnight

Calmly the night has come ashore;
she rests dreaming on the wall of the mountain.
Her eye now watches that the golden scales
of time rest quiet in even balance.
　And more boldly the fountains gush;
　they sing in the ear of the mother, night,
　of the day,
of the day that was today.

To the age-old slumber song
she doesn't listen, she is tired of it;
to her the blue heaven sounds sweeter still,
the even-slung yoke of the fleeting hours.
　Yet ever the fountains persist with the word,
　the waters sing continuously in sleep
　of the day,
of the day that was today.

Und willst du deinen Liebsten sterben sehen?

Und willst du deinen Liebsten sterben sehen,
So trage nicht dein Haar gelockt, du Holde.
Laβ von den Schultern frei sie niederwehen;
Wie Fäden sehn sie aus von purem Golde.
Wie goldne Fäden, die der Wind bewegt—
Schön sind die Haare, schön ist, die sie trägt!
Goldfäden, Seidenfäden ungezählt—
Schön sind die Haare, schön ist, die sie strählt!

Paul Johann Ludwig Heyse, 1830–1914 (from the Italian)

Verborgenheit

Laβ, o Welt, o laβ mich sein!
Locket nicht mit Liebesgaben,
Laβt dies Herz alleine haben
Seine Wonne, seine Pein!

Was ich traure, weiβ ich nicht,
Es ist unbekanntes Wehe;
Immerdar durch Tränen sehe
Ich der Sonne liebes Licht.

Oft bin ich mir kaum bewuβt,
Und die helle Freude zücket
Durch die Schwere, so mich drücket
Wonniglich in meiner Brust.

Laβ, o Welt, o laβ mich sein!
Locket nicht mit Liebesgaben,
Laβt dies Herz alleine haben
Seine Wonne, seine Pein!

Eduard Friedrich Mörike, 1804–75

*(Robert Franz, op. 28, no. 5; Franz Wüllner, op. 7, no. 4; Eduard
Lassen; others)*

And Would You See Your Lover Perish?

And would you see your lover perish?
Then do not wear your hair in curls, my dear.
Let it flow freely down around your shoulders—
seeming like threads of pure gold.
Like golden threads caressed by the wind—
beautiful hair, beautiful she who wears it!
Golden threads, silken threads—numberless—
beautiful hair, beautiful she who combs it!

Secrecy

Leave me to myself, o world!
Tempt me not with love-offerings;
let this heart have alone
its joy, its suffering!

Why I grieve I do not know,
it is some unknown pain:
always through my tears I see
the beloved light of the sun.

Often I hardly know myself,
and radiant joy flashes,
through the troubles that oppress me,
blissfully within my breast.

Leave me to myself, o world!
Tempt me not with love-offerings;
let this heart have alone
its joy, its suffering.

Das verlassne Mägdlein

Früh, wann die Hähne krähn,
Eh die Sternlein schwinden,
Muß ich am Herde stehn,
Muß Feuer zünden.

Schön ist der Flamme Schein,
Es springen die Funken.
Ich schaue so darein,
In Leid versunken.

Plötzlich, da kommt es mir,
Treuloser Knabe,
Daß ich die Nacht von dir
Geträumet habe!

Träne auf Träne dann
Stürzet hernieder;
So kommt der Tag heran—
O ging er wieder!

Eduard Friedrich Mörike, 1804–75

(Robert Schumann, op. 64, no. 2; Hans Pfitzner, op. 30, no. 2;
Ignaz Brüll, op. 5; Carl Reinecke, op. 19, no. 4; many others)

Verschwiegene Liebe

Über Wipfel und Saaten
In den Glanz hinein—
Wer mag sie erraten,
Wer holte sie ein?
Gedanken sich wiegen,
Die Nacht ist verschwiegen,
Gedanken sind frei.

The Forsaken Girl

Early, at cockcrow,
before the stars vanish,
I must be at the hearth,
I must light the fire.

The flames make a lovely light,
the sparks fly up;
I gaze at them
sunken in grief.

Suddenly I realize,
faithless boy,
that all night long
I have dreamed of you.

Tears upon tears then
fall;
so the day dawns—
O that it were over!

Secret Love

Over the treetops and the fields of grain,
in the moonlight—
who could guess them,
who overtake them?
Thoughts are in motion!
The night is silent,
thoughts are unconfined.

Errät es nur eine,
Wer an sie gedacht
Beim Rauschen der Haine,
Wenn niemand mehr wacht
Als die Wolken, die fliegen—
Mein Lieb ist verschwiegen
Und schön wie die Nacht.

Joseph, Freiherr von Eichendorff, 1788–1857

Wenn du zu den Blumen gehst

Wenn du zu den Blumen gehst,
Pflücke die schönsten, dich zu schmücken.
Ach, wenn du in dem Gärtlein stehst,
Müsstest du dich selber pflücken.

Alle Blumen wissen ja,
Dass du hold bist ohnegleichen.
Und die Blume, die dich sah,
Farb' und Schmuck muss ihr erbleichen.

Wenn du zu den Blumen gehst
Pflücke die schönsten, dich zu schmücken.
Ach, wenn du in dem Gärtlein stehst,
Müsstest du dich selber pflücken.

Lieblicher als Rosen sind
Die Küsse, die dein Mund verschwendet,
Weil der Reiz der Blumen endet
Wo dein Liebreiz erst beginnt.

Wenn du zu den Blumen gehst
Pflücke die schönsten, dich zu schmücken.
Ach, wenn du in dem Gärtlein stehst,
Müsstest du dich selber pflücken.

Paul Johann Ludwig Heyse, 1830–1914 (from the Spanish)

May only one guess
who is thinking of her,
in the rustling of the grove
when no one else is awake.
As the clouds that soar
my love is silent,
and lovely as the night.

When You Go among the Flowers

When you go among the flowers
pick the most beautiful to adorn yourself.
Ah, if you stand in the garden
it is yourself you must pick.

All the flowers know
that you are charming without rival,
and the flower that has seen you
must pale in color and adornment.

When you go among the flowers
pick the most beautiful to adorn yourself.
Ah, if you stand in the garden
it is yourself you must pick.

Lovelier than roses are
the kisses that your mouth lavishes,
for the charm of the flowers ends
where your love charm first begins.

When you go among the flowers
pick the most beautiful to adorn yourself.
Ah, when you stand in the garden
it is yourself you must pick.

Index of Composers

(Main sections are in italic.)

Index of Poets

Index of Titles and First Lines